# UNDERSTANDING REALISM

## Dedication

For the cast and crew
of *EastEnders*

# UNDERSTANDING REALISM

**Richard Armstrong**

**Series editor: Dr Stacey Abbott**

 Publishing

# Editor's Note

The moving image is now an integral part of our daily lives, representing an increasing share of our cultural activity. New generations of students know the moving image more intimately and more intensely than their predecessors – but they are not always well served in relating this experience to the academic study of film and television.

Understanding the Moving Image is a news series of short orientation texts in the formal study of screen media, with each book offering an introduction to one important topic. All the books will be written at an accessible level, with no assumption of prior academic knowledge on the part of the reader, by authors with teaching experience and an interest/specialism in a particular area.

As befitting a British Film Institute project, the series will privilege the study of the moving image – notably cinema and television. Case materials will focus on text familiar (and readily available) to the intended readership, without ducking the responsibility to raise awareness of longer traditions and broader horizons. All books will have a structure designed to facilitate learning for the individual reader, while remaining suitable for classroom seminar context.

The books will be useful to the following:
* Post-16 students working for examinations in media and film studies
* Course leaders and teachers from schools to first-year university and adult education
* The general reader with no prior background to the subject.

We are delighted to present the second book in the series, *Understanding Realism*, a fascinating exploration of the complex issues relating to realism in film and television.

Dr Stacey Abbott
**for British Film Institute 2005**
publishing@bfi.org.uk

First published in 2005 by the
British Film Institute
21 Stephen Street, London W1T 1LN
The British Film Institute offers you opportunities to experience,
enjoy and discover more about the world of film and television.

Designed, edited and set by Ampersand Publishing Services/Siobhán O'Connor, London
Cover design: Squid Inc./Jethro Clunies-Ross
Cover images: (front) *Kandahar* (Makhmalbaf Productions, 2001); *Double Indemnity*
(Paramount Pictures, 1944); *Cathy Come Home* (BBC, 1966); *The Bill* (Thames Television);
(back) *The Blair Witch Project* (Artisan Entertainment, 1999), courtesy of *bfi* Stills
Printed in Great Britain by Cromwell Press, Trowbridge, Wiltshire

British Library Cataloguing-in-Publication data
A catalogue record for this book is available from the British Library
ISBN 1-84457-062-2

# Preface

Appropriately enough for a book on the moving image and its interface with experience, the writing of *Understanding Realism* found me drawing on a number of real experiences. Examining the aesthetics of mainstream Hollywood and American independent cinema recalled ushering at the old Cambridge Arts Cinema as a student, and teaching Film Studies in adult education in the late 1990s. Writing about mainstream Hollywood, American independents and the various realisms of World Cinema brought to mind stints of film reviewing since the mid 1990s. Writing about soap opera saw me draw upon nightly experience of *EastEnders*, a series to which I became addicted.

The need to explain in detail how various aesthetics operate to generate simulacra of real experience has further reinforced my sense of the limitations of traditional film reviewing. It has also made me all the more aware of the complex contract that exists between moving image aesthetics and represented experience, and between spectators and the screen. In its attempt to explicate these relationships, I hope this book captures something of the excitement and pleasure which they can bring.

Myriad writers have assisted and flavoured my research, but I suspect my editor Andrew Lockett's unstinting enthusiasm, input and patience can be felt throughout the book. More recently, reader Dr Stacey Abbott of Roehampton University inflected and finessed this project with her valuable suggestions and assiduous feedback. I am grateful, too, to Siobhán O'Connor, for her feedback and design sense.

The scope of a book on realism in the moving image must of necessity be wide. I acknowledge the assistance of a number of specialists, among them Matthew Niednagel and Catalin Brylla at the Film-Philosophy chat room, and John Conomos for his work on the 'New Documentary' at that wonderful resource Senses of Cinema. I am grateful to all these individuals.

Richard Armstrong
October 2004

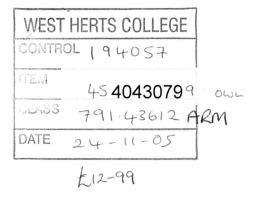

# Contents

# Introduction

The *Concise Oxford English Dictionary* defines 'realism' in its everyday sense as the 'practice of regarding things in their true nature and dealing with them as they are'. In its aesthetic sense, it is defined as 'fidelity to nature in representation; the showing of life etc as it is in fact'. These definitions assume that we live in a world full of things and experiences that have specific natures and that their natures are facts of life. But equally both assume that the nature of things can be represented. In 1913 a British newspaper famously ran the headline: 'FOG IN CHANNEL, CONTINENT ISOLATED.' A reasonable representation of adverse weather conditions, perhaps. But what headline would a French newspaper have run? Clearly, our representations of nature are shaped by factors other than the brute facticity, or material reality, of a thing – the fact of its being a fact in the world. *Understanding Realism* may help us to think about and use other concepts – representation, truth, ideology – in conjunction with realism.

If things are often not what they seem, neither is realism. Indeed, the very title of this book assumes that an explanation of at least this length is necessary in order to understand what on the face of it seems a fairly straightforward term. The fact is that, in the cinema, there is no such thing as realism per se. As I hope will become clear, there is no one realism. Realisms are relative, slipping in and out of and between other factors such as narrative, genre and audience in a film or television programme's bid to represent real experience. Rather than standing for a particular aesthetic, realism exists on a sort of

'From neo-realism to cinéma-vérité, film history has reliably proved authenticity is a chimerical goal. Sooner or later, the impression of raw immediacy congeals and stands exposed as a style like any other.' (Critic Peter Matthews in Sight and Sound *magazine, March 1999, p. 39*)

▶ Recall a film that struck you as realistic. Why was this? Now recall one that you did not find realistic. Why was this? ●

sliding scale, each gradation of which is defined more or less by the realism which came before and went after it. This book does not seek to identify a particular aesthetic. Rather, it aims to clarify the extent to which a film or television programme can be deemed realist and what role our perception of textual realism plays in our understanding of a text.

Realism is a fascinating topic. Indeed, I am writing this book on the assumption that no more ambiguous or dangerous term exists in Film and Media Studies. Realism is founded on a contradiction, and to understand it is to realize that what you are watching is as much *representation* as represented. At the core of the term may be some agreement between text and spectator about the nature of the real – just as I assume there is between you and me. But you and I cannot afford to ignore the fact that there are two parts to the term realism. Its root refers to the real, the thing represented, while 'ism' calls to mind realism's status as a mode of representing. Just as expressionism and impressionism are modes and movements of representation, realism is as much about traditions, modes and strategies of representation as it is about what they represent. This book will draw your attention to the methods by which particular types of film, whether Hollywood or US independent, comedies or documentaries, *EastEnders* or *Rome, Open City*, construct models of the real. Chapters 2 to 5 are each built around a particular example of film-making practice from mainstream Hollywood to British TV realism.

A film's realism depends upon the industrial context in which it was made, the cultural context in which it was received, and you and me as members of the audience. Among the questions I would like to ask of a film are those which coalesce around the industrial context. How does a Hollywood film's genre shape its realism? How is Hollywood's 'reality effect' marketed? Are the loose ends we find in American independent films more realistic than Hollywood's happy endings? What level of realism do we expect from foreign-language films? What ideas about reality and real experience do *you* bring to a film or TV programme? *Understanding Realism* is necessarily short, so in order to expand discussion the comments, questions, activities and commentary in the margins are designed to get you thinking about your viewing experiences from different directions, as it were, and how they and this book might interact.

Films get made because someone points a camera at a scene and shoots. From the biggest, most commercial Hollywood movie to the smallest no-budget webcam short, all moving-image texts involve a set of decisions about what to shoot, how long to shoot and when to cut. Film-makers *make* films. When Francis Ford Coppola went to the Philippines in the 1970s he came back with *Apocalypse Now* (1979), a very different film from *Full Metal Jacket*, the film Stanley Kubrick made in 1987. Both are films about the Vietnam War. Both fall to one extent or another under the banner of realism. But realism is a moveable feast, and it is a measure of its richness that one experience can generate three very different takes, each shaped by the concerns of an industry, an audience and an individual film-maker. The films I have chosen to focus upon in detail illustrate the degree to which there is no such thing as realism. There are only realisms. As the films which are discussed in detail are very enjoyable and widely available on DVD or video, it is strongly recommended that you watch them in conjunction with reading the book.

# 1. What Is Realism?

*This chapter describes cinematic realism emerging from the realist tradition in western philosophy and the arts in which experience and artifice played equal roles. Tracing realist and anti-realist tendencies in cinema, the chapter questions the status of experience and representation in realist films. Notions of 'reality effects' and 'truth effects' are introduced to account for the represented/representation conundrum.*

The Belgian Surrealist painter René Magritte painted a number of canvases depicting a smoking pipe beneath which ran the statement 'Ceci n'est pas une pipe' ('This is not a pipe'). Above the words is an almost photographic painting of a pipe. These paintings express one of this elusive artist's most accessible ideas because, by playing with the differing natures of images and the words that describe them, Magritte's message is clear. Images of real objects *are* simply images. We may point at the picture and say 'pipe', yet still it remains not a real pipe, but a representation of a pipe. Magritte's message gets to the bottom of the issue of realism.

   Realism seeks to depict real objects and experience. But the term is as much about representation as it is about reality. The *Concise Oxford English Dictionary* defines 'representation' as 'an image, likeness, or reproduction of a thing, e.g. a painting or drawing' – or a film or a TV programme. Watching a Los Angeles homicide cop chasing his man in the Hollywood thriller *Heat* (Michael Mann, 1995), we are actually watching a series of images, pieces of celluloid edited together in a

*'A film is hundreds of moments photographed and joined together to create an illusion of something which did not take place.' (Film director Michael Winner, quoted by Poppy and Stevenson in* Realism, Film Education, *1998, p. 1)*

Heat: *Just pieces of celluloid edited together . . .*

▶ Think of films that encourage you to see what goes on in them in a particular way. Why do we see the Lumière employees approaching the camera rather than leaving it in *Workers Leaving the Factory*? Why do Melanie and Jack in *One Fine Day* constantly find themselves in close proximity? ●

particular way to represent a detective pursuing a suspect somewhere in present-day Los Angeles. When we see Andie MacDowell, a real individual, chatting to a friend in *The Player* (Robert Altman, 1992), we are watching a series of images – pieces of film – edited together in a certain way to represent a real person's actions. This is an image of a particular individual who genuinely exists, but the image of her is shaped by the way in which the film has been shot and edited. This is *not* Andie MacDowell. These are images of Andie MacDowell. Even the workers whom we see leaving the factory in the Lumière brothers' film *Workers Leaving the Factory* (1895) are not real. However 'raw' and 'gritty' we say this footage is – and indeed other realist films are – it is still only a representation of this event. Cinema pioneers widely regarded as having invented moving pictures, the Lumières began their film with the opening of the factory gates and ended it with the closing of the gates, thus framing apparently random experiences so as to lend the film narrative some shape. The bottom line is that when you watch a film or TV programme, you are watching nothing but a representation of reality. This is what films and television programmes are. But what happened to *realism*? Why Italian neo-*realism*? Why '*reality* TV'? To answer these questions we must begin by going back to well before the cinema was invented.

## The real world and the ideal world

For centuries philosophers have argued about how we know what we know about the world. One faction has argued that there are material things existing in space and time independently of the individual's knowledge of them. I only know that things exist in space and time when evidence reaches me via the data that I perceive through my senses. For example, I know that there is a bird in the tree because I hear its song. I know that I have left the oven switched on without lighting it because I can smell gas. But that bird and that gas leak could exist independently of what I perceive about them. They could exist even though I am not here. The other philosophical faction has argued that things do not in themselves exist in space and time. They exist only as ideas that I have of them. Thus I infer the existence of songbirds and gas leaks from the ideas that I have of these things. Take me away from the birdsong and the smell of gas and they may just as well not exist.

These two ways of thinking have had major impacts on the arts. The materialist assumption was at the heart of nineteenth-century realism. Reacting against the Romantic movement of the late eighteenth and early nineteenth centuries, which held that ideas govern how we experience the world, the materialist assumption had been translated into a widespread and influential set of aims and methods by the 1850s. Theorists and practitioners in art, fiction and drama developed techniques for the thorough and accurate representation of experience in all its social and domestic variety. Artists Gustave Courbet and Hilaire Degas created a realm of things and experiences in the real world. The work of both of them embodies the essential contradiction found within realism. Courbet and Degas were also influenced by photography, a new art form emerging in the mid nineteenth century, and Degas's work anticipated the era's experiments in motion photography. Yet Degas's paintings were in fact

▶ Do you think we still believe in a truth that exists irrespective of what you or I, or a film director or a news reporter, as individuals experience? Relate an experience you have had to a friend, then relate the same experience to another friend in writing. ●

Derived from the work of French theatre and film director André Antoine, who insisted on location shooting, multi-camera point-of-view and editing which made the spectator identify with the camera, cinematic naturalism brings the spectator into all-too-human stories. It works to involve us as bystanders much as the audiences of boxing movies such as *Ali* (Michael Mann, 2001) 'naturalize' the position of bystander by making us identify with the audience at a boxing match. But what values are made to seem natural in Hollywood films?

scrupulously composed. This interaction between experience and personal expression is at the heart of artistic, literary and cinematic realism.

The description of a society evolving in space and time emerges in French novelist Honoré de Balzac's almost sociological accounts of Parisian social classes in the 1830s and 1840s, through Flaubert's realist milestone *Madame Bovary* (1857), to the extreme realism, or 'naturalism', of Emile Zola in the 1880s and 1890s. Flaubert's *Madame Bovary* is a key realist work. That it has been filmed three times reveals something about the cinema's perennial identification with literary realism, and its concern with aesthetics. Detailing the romantic aspirations and disappointments of a young married woman, Flaubert caught both the brute facticity of the fleeting moment and the way in which events reach us in terms of how individuals see them. *Madame Bovary* seemed to emerge out of life as we tend to experience it, relayed to us not just by our senses, but also by our opinions and prejudices and the opinions and prejudices of others. Theorists have written that realism is never a formless mass of unmediated experience. It must have certain logical structures. As we look at Hollywood, US independent, British cinema, art cinema and documentary, we shall become aware of the structures, techniques and devices with which these distinctive aesthetics shape experience.

Dominant among the 'voices' we hear in *Madame Bovary* is Emma's own naive and romantic point of view. What distinguishes the various realisms that we will be looking at in chapters 4 and 5 is an issue related to where raw experience can be found, where the director's representation of experience ends, and where a character's viewpoint begins. Many of the decisions made about how experience is represented have to do with whose story is being told. Flaubert wanted to catch the experience as mediated by the individual *and* to clinically report the unvarnished detail. But are not even Flaubert's most strenuous efforts to be clinical themselves the result of his specific way of seeing, with all the baggage which goes with a point of view? Film directors, too, are constantly caught between levels of representation. The staunchest Italian neo-realist film is torn between the brute facticity of the streets and the attitudes and opinions of those who live there. While Rossellini's very decision to film on the streets of Rome in *Rome, Open City* (Roberto Rossellini, 1945) brings home the air and atmosphere of a particular place, it also brings with it Rossellini's own assumptions about the nature of experience. Realism is a conundrum.

The development of photography from 1839 onwards saw painting drift away from the mimetic, or exact copy of experience, and towards the examination of its own methods, a shift which led eventually to the depiction of light itself in the work of the impressionists. Work such as Pierre Auguste Renoir's *Le Déjeuner des canotiers* (1881) and Claude Monet's paintings of water lilies (1903–23) is typical of this shift. With the benefit of hindsight, it is easy to see how photography and cinematography could have emerged during an era so preoccupied with realism. While it is true that photography was able to record images of the world with infinitely greater clarity than painting, it was nevertheless quickly recognized that any intervention by the photographer between the camera and the world introduced aesthetics to photography. Did one 'take' a photograph or 'make' a photograph? The nineteenth-century debate surrounding photography as a record and as an art led to differing strands in photographic aesthetics that would resonate in the early development of cinematography. If by 1848 realism had become the most important movement in French art and literature, by 1850 photographers had begun to think about introducing motion into the photographic image. It was only a matter of time before the motion picture camera would capture experience in *all* its fluid detail. The moving picture would give rise to a whole new set of aesthetics.

▶ Pick up a camera and point it at something. Are you 'taking' or 'making' this photograph? ●

## What is cinematic realism?

The history of film aesthetics is often thought of in terms of the evolution and interaction of two tendencies. In December 1895 moving pictures were first shown publicly by photographic entrepreneurs the brothers Lumière (Louis and Auguste) in Paris. These '*actualités*' (literally, 'current events') were real events filmed as they actually happened. *Workers Leaving the Factory* and *Arrival of a Train at La Ciotat Station* (1895) are simply filmed records of employees leaving the Lumière factory at the end of the day and the arrival of a train, respectively. Recording everyday events and shot at eye

Workers Leaving the Factory: *The nitty gritty of everyday life*

*Méliès'* A Trip to the Moon *(1904): Turning experience into a trick*

▶ Have you ever watched a film in which ordinary people do ordinary things and been riveted by it? Why was this the case? ●

*Industry professionals working in film and TV refer to live footage as 'actualities', or 'acts', as in the Acts of the Apostles, which have had the reputation of being absolutely true for centuries.*

*'With Lumière, trains entered stations, with Méliès they got off the rails and flew into the clouds.' (Film historian Claude Beylie (1932–2001), quoted by Ginette Vincendeau in the Encyclopedia of European Cinema, Vincendeau (ed.), Cassell, 1995, p. 285)*

*French film theorist André Bazin (1918–58) traced the history of the cinema in terms of its gradual achievement of realism.*

level with unobtrusive editing and no camera movement, these films are the earliest examples of cinematic realism, and enthralled audiences wherever they were shown. Related to realism in painting and literature through their preoccupation with ordinary experience and unadorned style, the Lumière films embody a key pattern underlying the evolution of film.

The other tendency is represented most famously by the work of Georges Méliès. *Un Voyage dans la lune* (*A Trip to the Moon*, 1902) remains the most celebrated example of his work, a fantasy about a rocket journey to the moon. Méliès is considered the inventor of the 'trick film', in which the visual gimmickry of the theatre was augmented with such cinematic trickery as jump cuts, whereby a cut occurs in the middle of an action being shot, creating a 'jump' in the action. Méliès also employed double exposures, in which two images are superimposed on the same piece of film. Unlike the Lumière brothers, Méliès' work relied upon what film aesthetics brought to the representation of experience.

It is possible to trace Lumière realism and Méliès trickery throughout film history by examining the degree to which a film reveals real experience and the degree to which it uses filmic techniques to shape these depictions. However, the issue of realism is also subject to historical circumstance. Sometimes sped up, sometimes run backwards, even the apparently self-evident Lumière films could be seen more as spectacle by contemporary audiences. So our ideas of what is realistic closely relate to the conventions of representation to which we are accustomed. While these conventions change over time, we now see realisms as distinct moments on a sliding scale. Indeed, all films exist at some point or another along a scale something like the one below.

You might argue that *EastEnders* and *The Full Monty* (Peter Cattaneo, 1997) belong to the Lumière end of the scale because they seem to record the nitty gritty of everyday life. You could argue that *Lara Croft: Tomb Raider* (Simon West, 2001) and *A Matter of Life and Death* (Michael Powell & Emeric Pressburger, 1946) belong to the Méliès end because they depict fantasy worlds. Theorists have written that Méliès' experiments laid the groundwork for the 'cinema of attractions', that brand of film which, like *Tomb Raider*, makes you gasp at the possibilities of cinematic spectacle. But a film such as *Speed* (Jan de Bont, 1994) complicates the situation. Its scenario is patently far-fetched, relying upon editing for its effects. Yet it also transparently takes place in a contemporary Los Angeles which we recognize either because we have seen it in documentaries or news items or because we may actually have been there. But what are we to make of a bus flying through the air and landing safely fifty feet away?

So the Lumière and Méliès tendencies interact as well as separately evolve. Supposedly realist and supposedly anti-realist films are each interpenetrated by aesthetics and experience. Even the Lumières made a range of decisions about how they wanted experience to appear, displaying a remarkable understanding of what cinematic technique brings to depictions of the real. And let's not forget that, for all their 'realism', the Lumière films were shot without sound

▶ Construct a realist sliding scale like the one below using other films that you have seen. ●

The 'cinema of attractions' is a term first coined by film historian Tom Gunning in his essay 'The Cinema of Attractions: Early Film, its Spectator, and the Avant-Garde', which can be found in *Early Cinema: Space, Frame, Narrative*, Thomas Elsaesser (ed.), BFI Publishing, 1990.

▶ To take an example from the Lumière end of the scale, what are we to make of those moments in *One Fine Day* when two people appear to be having a phone conversation with each other in the same shot? ●

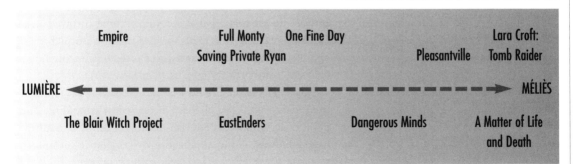

| | | | | | Lara Croft: |
| Empire | Full Monty | One Fine Day | | | Tomb Raider |
| | Saving Private Ryan | | Pleasantville | | |

LUMIÈRE ◀ ─ ─ ─ ─ ─ ─ ─ ─ ─ ─ ─ ─ ─ ─ ─ ─ ─ ─ ─ ─ ─ ─ ─ ─ ─ ─ ─ ▶ MÉLIÈS

| The Blair Witch Project | EastEnders | Dangerous Minds | A Matter of Life and Death |

and in black-and-white. At the other end of the scale, the heroine of *Lara Croft: Tomb Raider – The Cradle of Life* (Jan de Bont, 2003) embodies attitudes of resilience and self-determination widely shared among real young women in the 1990s and 2000s.

So if the idea of realism untouched by technique and anti-realism untouched by experience is difficult to envisage, are the Lumière and Méliès models still useful ways to talk about moving images? Yes, I think they are, if only because the search for more poignant ways of capturing real experience is as old as cinema itself. One account of the evolution of Hollywood cinema is based upon technologies of image and sound enhancement. According to this history, in 1927 sound was added to the image with the arrival of 'talkies'. In the 1930s and 1940s 'deep focus' cinematography enhanced the amount of space and time that could be included in a single shot. In the 1950s widescreen techniques enhanced the spectator's illusion of being immersed in the film. In the late 1940s, rising costs and falling income drove Hollywood studios to film on location. By the mid 1950s more and more Hollywood films were being shot in colour. In the 1960s and 1970s, stereophonic and quadraphonic sound were, like colour, part of the industry's attempt to provide an increasingly realistic experience. Yet at the same time there is an element of spectacle to all these technologies which inevitably makes them all components of Hollywood's showmanship.

## 'Reality effects' and 'truth effects'

Given how complex an issue the representation of reality seems to be, perhaps it is more helpful to look at the depiction of experience in films in terms of effects. When we go to the cinema, we do not go expecting to see real events. But we do go hoping that we will become involved in an experience that seems real. Another method of quantifying and qualifying the extent of a text's realism is by thinking in terms of 'reality effects' and 'truth effects'.

Reality effects signify how far representations in a moving image text mimic the facticity of the world around us. They have to do with surface verisimilitude. A bit of a mouthful, 'verisimilitude' is the appearance or semblance of truth or reality in a text. It is used to measure how authentic the world

▶ Hollywood has been at the forefront of technologies of image and sound enhancement. What reasons can you think of for this being so? ●

'Practically, totally real. But not.' Lois Kaiser in Short Cuts (Robert Altman, 1993)

of a film or television programme is. For example, in *Heat* the homicide cop works the neighbourhoods of downtown Los Angeles. What would you think if you saw him chasing his prey amid a raft of red London double-deckers going about their business? It is highly likely this would jar with your belief in what you are seeing. And if the reality effect of authentic LA street life is disturbed, it becomes difficult for spectators to take on trust what they see. Their attention will drift and perhaps make them question other aspects of the film, until they become increasingly distracted from involvement by the lack of verisimilitude. Equally, if the Slater family in *EastEnders* began talking with Merseyside accents, while on Channel 4 the characters of the soap opera *Brookside* had Cockney accents, this would violate our perception that these characters do not, and should not, sound like this. These issues would interfere with our viewing pleasure and the texts' credibility.

Truth effects signify how far representations chime with our ideas of what is true about the world in a general sense. More abstract than the exact verisimilitude of this or that surface detail, truth effects have to do with whether texts conform to what we generally believe about experience. For example, when watching *Heat* we expect to see unsavoury characters and violent acts represented because these chime with a widely held sense of the kind of people with whom the LA homicide bureau are likely to come into contact. When we watch *EastEnders* and everyone speaks with Cockney accents, this, too, chimes with our perception that this is how natives of London's East End really sound.

But the realism of this or that text is also related to a number of other factors. Surface verisimilitude differs from one member of an audience to the next according to the text and the audience member. An old soldier may notice that in *Saving Private Ryan* (Steven Spielberg, 1998) the wrong cap badges are used in one scene, whereas for a young couple in the next row this may not matter. Our ideas of what is realistic also change from era to era. If a character is shot nowadays, we expect to see lots of blood because we know from news coverage that real violence is bloody. New technology rewrites the rules by which a film can be described as 'realist'. For example, digital video (DV) is currently considered to seem more 'realistic' than film. We like to think that some

In his book *Visible Fictions*, theorist John Ellis talks about **codes**, each with distinct criteria, through which we can tease forth reality and truth effects. These codes include that of verisimilitude, a way of gauging the surface reality of a film or TV programme's world. Another code gauges the realism of psychology or character motivation. Still another asks if a text constructs a compelling and persuasive sense of truth. In other words, these codes make for a more 'scientific' rationale for our perception of reality and truth effects.

*The issue of what narratives are most realistic is important to cinematic realisms. The everyday world of work is commonly depicted in films such as* One Fine Day, Clerks *and* Dangerous Minds, *all of which take place in the workaday world.*

See Chapter 4 to find out how 'street realism' fits into *Dangerous Minds'* pitch to its audience.

narratives are more realistic than others. We tend to think soap operas are more lifelike than romantic comedies. What is the relationship between realism and genre? Some music videos, for example, generate a particular type of 'street realism', one that the credit sequence of *Dangerous Minds* (John M. Smith, 1995) plays with, as we shall see. What role do governments, studios, censors play in shaping realism? All these issues will be discussed in the next two chapters.

# 2. Narrative and Realism

*This chapters looks at how the Hollywood movie operates to create the illusion of reality, examining the role of narrative, editing, characterization and the soundtrack in this process. By comparison, we examine how these criteria work in the US independent film's take on experience. We will also trace the evolution of the Hollywood soundtrack. Finally, the Hollywood mode is contrasted with those film-making strategies that have drawn attention to the illusory methods of mainstream film-making.*

## Classical realist narrative

The classical realist narrative forms the essential structure of the nineteenth-century novel, the Hollywood film and television drama. It is organized around three dramatic shifts: a) a situation is established; b) the situation is disrupted; and c) the disruption is resolved and a fresh situation brought into being. In *Madame Bovary* we are presented with a young married couple starting life in a small Normandy village where Charles Bovary practises medicine. Emma Bovary is happy, until she becomes bored with this life, begins to run up bills and has affairs. She falls into debt and poisons herself, and Charles is left alone in the village. This simple structure was in evidence in many films from the early cinema period and has endured into the contemporary original screenplay, dominating the bulk of what we watch today.

In the Hollywood romantic comedy *One Fine Day* (Michael Hoffman, 1996) Melanie is a divorced single parent whose life

*'There's only one way to shoot a scene, and that's the way which shows the audience what's happening next.'*
*(Director Raoul Walsh, quoted by Bordwell, 1985, p. 30)*

In a famous essay theorist Colin MacCabe wrote:
*The narrative prose achieves its position of dominance because it is in the position of knowledge and this function of knowledge is taken up in the cinema by the narration of events. Through the knowledge we gain from the narrative we can split the discourses of the various characters from their situation and compare what is said in these discourses with what has been revealed to us through narration. The camera shows us what happens – it tells the truth against which we can measure the other discourses.'* (*Realism in the Cinema: Notes on Some Brechtian Theses*, 1974, p.10)
Writing about the Hollywood thriller *Klute* (Alan J. Pakula, 1971), MacCabe shows how the film's soundtrack may suggest a particular ending, but the true ending is revealed in what we see happen.

▶ Can you think of another film in which there was a discrepancy between what you were told and what you saw? ●

revolves around her son, Sammy, and her career. Owing to circumstances beyond her control, one day her life must revolve around Jack, another divorced single parent. By the end of the day, both their lives have been disrupted, but they have saved their careers and fallen in love. In *EastEnders*, Anthony was going to marry Zoe, but then Zoe ran away from home. When Anthony and Zoe's mother, Kat, searched for her they became close and slept together. Unable to deal with his disappointment, guilt and confusion, Anthony left Albert Square to go on a holiday to Antigua. The story strand began with a couple on the verge of marriage, then one of them left and the other had an affair, and a fresh situation came into being. The resolution of the classic realist narrative finds the characters a little wiser for their experiences and, supposedly, living happily ever after in a new situation. Joining the three parts of the narrative together is a series of causes and effects that lead logically on from one another so that the progression from the original situation to the final resolution is believable and seems realistic.

In both the Hollywood film and the TV soap opera the camerawork and editing 'follow' the story in a logical way so as to generate the impression that life is being shown as it really is. But this impression is an illusion. This is borne in on you when you stop to consider how dialogue-driven *One Fine Day* and *EastEnders* are. In a dialogue-driven Hollywood movie such as *One Fine Day*, dialogue is not simply a device for moving the story forward. It is also, in its literate and humorous way, a production value, part of the entertainment provided by the movie. And in this way it disrupts the illusion of the everyday that *One Fine Day* presumes to generate. Unfortunately, what real people say is seldom as literate or funny as this. While conversation drives the plot along in *EastEnders*, it also foregrounds disputes and crises, the stuff of soap opera plotting, over all the ephemeral and 'plotless' dialogue real people engage in. Notice, too, that nobody stutters, fumbles with their words or speaks with their mouths full in Albert Square. The disruption of the cause-and-effect chain also interferes with the illusion of realism. *The Man Who Wasn't There* (Joel Coen, 2001), for example, left audiences wondering why the hero's wife, who has committed suicide in prison, turns up on his doorstep. Musicals were an important part of Hollywood's output in the past, but you might ask according to what narrative logic do characters suddenly burst into song!

You will remember how a classic realist novel such as *Madame Bovary* was composed of two narrative zones. One consisted of the voices and opinions of various characters; the other consisted of Flaubert's 'metalanguage' objectively describing what happens, where it happens and so on. In nineteenth-century realism language is used to report subjective opinions, *and* to objectively describe characters and scenes. In the Hollywood film these functions are carried out through dialogue and images. Yet, as we saw in Chapter 1, nothing we see should challenge the reality effect. It is as if when we see Melanie coping with Sammy and her career, meeting and dealing with journalist Jack, and falling in love with him, we are witnessing part of a real individual's life, a life that began before the film began and will continue after the film has finished.

## Classical Hollywood matchmaking

> *'This isn't some horrifyingly elaborate*
> *matchmaking scheme, is it?'*

In a Hollywood film such as *One Fine Day*, style must be subordinate to the film's narrative. No aspect of the way in which the film tells its story must get in the way of our ability to follow the story itself. This means that camerawork, editing, lighting and colour must serve the storyline, place you in the most advantageous position to see what is going on and banish any doubt about what you see. There must be no weird angles, choppy cutting or strange lens filters to make you aware of the film as a *film*, as opposed to real life, for Hollywood realism is designed to make you think that life is how it looks in the movies; however, *One Fine Day* is quite old-fashioned in this regard. 'Post-classical' Hollywood films have made more of the interface between style and narrative, as we shall see.

What are most Hollywood films about? The overwhelming majority of Hollywood films contain what is known in Hollywood committee rooms and in critical circles as 'love interest', a scenario which, however subsidiary to the action movie, courtroom drama or crime thriller logic of the film, involves a heterosexual relationship. And in dealing with this theme they make love seem like something that happens every day. Hollywood films employ a range of techniques to

▶ Can you recall a film that seemed to deliberately stop 'making sense'? Did you switch it off, or did you continue to watch? Why was this? ●

*When they were researching their important book* The Classical Hollywood Cinema, *authors Bordwell, Staiger and Thompson reckoned that 95 out of 100 films they had chosen to discuss involved romantic love. The other line of action in the Hollywood film involves a work-related goal, the writers stipulate. This could be 'business, spying, sports, politics, crime, show business' (p. 16) — or, presumably, journalism or architectural design.*

make the match between story experience and real experience apparently seamless because Hollywood wants you to escape into the story. By doing so, Hollywood films make the idea of romantic love seem natural, an everyday event. It is going to happen to everyone sooner or later. Unfolding according to the formula 'boy meets girl/boy loses girl/boy gets girl', Hollywood films adhere to a tradition going all the way back to medieval literature. On the level of reality effect, this formula is made to seem inevitable as one event smoothly follows the last according to the logic of verisimilitude and cause-and-effect. On the level of truth effects, this structure appeals to the romantic notion that there is someone in the world for everyone. And the intertwining of this romantic narrative with a vocational narrative thread in many Hollywood films appeals to a traditional perception that a young man should work hard and make good, readying himself to meet someone, marry and provide for a family.

Although they have emerged out of very different film-making traditions, *One Fine Day* and *Clerks* (Kevin Smith, 1993), which is discussed in detail later, both revolve around love and work. But what do these films' very distinctive qualities reveal about these experiences?

## One Fine Day

*'You know, I have a day.'*

*One Fine Day* is a mainstream romantic comedy starring Michelle Pfeiffer and George Clooney. Executive-produced by Pfeiffer, an established star since the 1980s, it was intended to be a 'star vehicle' that would advance relative newcomer Clooney's career. Conventional in its plotting, editing and characterization, the film exemplifies Hollywood's traditional brand of realism, its distinctive filmic match with experience reflected in the natural-seeming matchmaking of the plot.

Realism is part experience, part aesthetic, with each part interpenetrated by the other. *One Fine Day* charts the unfolding of an apparently typical day for Manhattan working people Melanie Parker and Jack Taylor. Like your day and my day, their day is structured around hours and minutes, a pattern mirrored by the film which is structured around time checks based on Jack's digital alarm clock: 6:30, 9:28, 1:59, 5:05. Yet as real as this day seems, we do not know which day it is. Like Melanie and Jack, we are used to measuring our day in hours and minutes. Yet we need to know whether it is Tuesday today or Thursday today because our schedule depends upon it. Again, that old realist conundrum. This is another working day in midtown Manhattan split into twenty-four hours, measured in minutes and divided by mealtimes. Yet these are not our hours and minutes. And this is not Tuesday or Thursday, or even Monday, because we are never told what day it is. This is 'any day'. On the one hand, the film wants us to think this is a typical Manhattan day unfolding as we watch. On the other, actual Manhattan days have names and dates. This particular occasion occurs on no calendar ever printed. It occurs outside history, if you like. This tells us a lot about the way in which Hollywood films work. While the Hollywood narrative is organized so that we follow characters as they pursue their goals, the bigger, historical picture against which backdrop their exploits take place, is simply that, a backdrop. Because we do not know what day it is or what the date is, *One Fine Day* offers no connections between the events taking place in Melanie and Jack's lives and events unfolding in the wider world. On real-life days we experience complex causes and outcomes. Reality is *much* more complex than the lives of any individual man and woman. The sinking of the *Titanic*, for example, was the result of a complex history of design and chance in which many individuals played a role. Yet the Hollywood film *Titanic* (James Cameron, 1997) concentrated on the stories of a handful of mainly fictitious people, in particular two lovers (Surprise, surprise!). *Saving Private Ryan* takes place during the Allied invasion of Nazi-occupied France in the summer of 1944. Yet the film revolves around a fictitious American officer and his unit's attempt to find one soldier out of thousands. Hollywood films are character-led. History is a weave of causes and effects, and is actually a bit more complicated than my, or your, everyday personal histories.

*One Fine Day* is a clever conceit. It seeks to mirror the spontaneous and provisional ways in which daily experiences occur: plans laid, plans changed, time lost, time gained. Yet every shot and cut has been thought through and finely executed. The producers obviously want you to think that these people are caught on the hop in real, verifiable New York locations. But if the locations are real, everything that

> The American thriller *Double Indemnity* (Billy Wilder, 1944) is set in May 1938, in the depths of the Great Depression. Yet no mention is made of the slump, while all the characters are employed and apparently affluent. On the other hand, the clothes they wear and the cars they drive place the action in the mid 1940s, when the film appeared, and at the height of World War II. Yet no mention is made of the war.
>
> ▶ Can you think of any reason why these major circumstances might be absent from the drama? ●

happens there has actually been planned beforehand. The producers want you to think that this is just another spring day for Melanie and Jack. You know that, of course. But this is also a day neither Melanie nor Jack will forget. How often does that happen – be honest. Hollywood aesthetics make a romantic comedy look like history, and history look like a romantic comedy. That's an assignment even trickier than saving your career and falling in love in one day!

## Editing

Hollywood editing is designed to follow the logic of a chronological narrative. In Hollywood 'continuity editing' as it is called, one plot twist follows on from the last according to the laws of cause and effect. Time and space are logically presented so as to orient you in an apparently natural sequence of events. After Jack's ex-wife, Kristen, gives him Melanie Parker's name because he needs a babysitter, Jack meets Melanie. This scene unfolds according to the standard Hollywood shot/reverse-shot format. As Jack speaks to Melanie, we see Jack over Melanie's shoulder. We then see Melanie over Jack's shoulder as she replies. It is as though Jack speaks to you, the spectator, when he faces the camera. It is as though Melanie speaks to you, the spectator, when she faces the camera. Yet because we seem to hover at the listener's shoulder, we are never completely cut off from them. In this way we are given privileged access to what's going on, but invited at the same time to share a character's perspective. At the start of the scene we see the two children Sammy and Maggie glaring at one another, seeming to set the tone of the scene between their parents. Such editing naturalizes, or puts you in the situation you are following. Shot/reverse-shot editing assists in us seeming to actually experience what the characters experience in their world by showing them interacting in such a way that we can easily follow the conversation and so follow the plot.

Editing is also organized so as not to violate your understanding of where you are in relation to a character. Hollywood films employ what is known as the 180-degree rule, whereby a hypothetical line drawn between two or more actors keeps the camera to one side of the action. If several shots of differing distances or angles are cut together, your perspective remains the same. Notice how the camera

One Fine Day's *Melanie and Jack are brought together through the use of shot/reverse shot*

remains to one side of Melanie and Jack when they first meet so that she is on the right and he on the left. We are then clear about how the shot/reverse-shot sequence proceeds. If the camera crossed this imaginary line, the characters would appear to have swapped sides of the frame and the backdrop will have altered, disorientating us. Later, when Jack dashes on to the Circle Line boat, the film cuts to the elderly passengers as they appear to Jack. It is obvious, then, that these people are on the boat. That you see them, rather than seeing Jack looking at them, makes you see the world of the film at this point through Jack's eyes. You therefore share in his disappointed realization that he is on the wrong boat and that Sammy's Circle Line boat has already left.

Hollywood editing is often referred to as 'invisible editing' because it helps the narrative along, without distracting us. We are in effect too busy following the narrative to notice the editing. It is a long and hallowed Hollywood method and, overall, *One Fine Day* follows the rules of invisible editing. Yet the cleverness with which the film has persuaded us that this apparently ordinary day is far from just another day is hinted at in some tricky editing. For example, did you notice that cut from Melanie's to Jack's alarm clock radio as both hit 6.30 near the beginning? *One Fine Day* also employs editing devices that seem to contradict the reality effect completely.

The split-screen effects in *One Fine Day* divide the image into two or more separate images that are not superimposed. The split screen is a device that has come in and out of practice, but here the producers wished to recall the split screens of romantic comedies of the 1930s, 1940s and 1950s. At various times we see Melanie and Jack talking to each other and to other characters such as Jack's editor Lew, Melanie's mother Rita and Jack's colleague Celia in split-screen compositions. This makes no logical sense, of course. We know we cannot really see the person we are speaking to on the phone. So why do these scenes not interrupt the flow? I suspect because, if I heard Lew or Rita's voices in voice-over coming out of thin air, rather than saw the character as they spoke, I would need a moment to adjust to whose voice this is. And that would jar and interrupt this speedy film. This device means that I am able instantly to recall these characters in the narrative space where I have seen them

▶ What do you think of the idea that shot/reverse-shot editing naturalizes the drama? Try to imagine an alternative to this method. ●

*Jack and Melanie in* One Fine Day: *split screen finds love triumphing over space and time*

The split-screen effect was traditionally associated with romantic comedy. Look out for *Pillow Talk* (Michael Gordon, 1959). Since the 1960s, however, multi-imaging has been used in other sorts of movies. *The Thomas Crown Affair* (Norman Jewison, 1968), *Phone Booth* (Joel Schumacher, 2002) and the TV series *24* (2001) are slick examples of contemporary multi-imaging.

▶ Is the 'shaping' work of film aesthetics becoming more obvious? ●

▶ *Double Indemnity* was considered revolutionary because it was built around a series of flashbacks. Filmic techniques work if they are well motivated by the plot. Consider a good flashback movie you have seen. Ask yourself why it works so well. ●

▶ Were you drawn into the story of *One Fine Day*? ●

before – newspaper office, cosmetics parlour – because I have already encountered them as people, not just as voices.

While shot/reverse-shot editing sets up the impression that you are 'listening in' on a conversation, fades and dissolves signal transitions between scenes, and montages give the impression of a series of events or the passage of time, other editing tricks have the effect of disrupting the reality effect. We have already seen how jump cuts disrupt the illusion, but rapid cutting can also bewilder the spectator. Expressive montage, a mode of rapid cutting seeming to build the film out of separate short shots as opposed to longer takes, was employed in Russian films of the 1920s to make an intellectual point in the midst of the action. Flashbacks and flash-forwards can disrupt the action by introducing past or future events into the present. Inserts, too, tend to disrupt the narrative, recalling mental processes in a character such as memories or visions which, although often explicable, tend to jar with the spectator following a present tense narrative. Avant-garde or 'oppositional' cinemas deploy a whole battery of editing effects such as awkward dissolves, 'automatic' shots in which the camera reveals random, irrational juxtapositions and superimpositions which disrupt. With Hollywood editing, the bottom line is always putting you in the most advantageous spot to see who is doing what. What is powerful about filmic conventions is that they naturalize particular ways of showing, and making sense of, experience.

### Characterization

The rules of Hollywood characterization traditionally dictate that characters are typed by occupation with particular traits added. So boxers tends to be tough but stupid. Teachers tend to be poor but idealistic. Newspaper editors tend to be grumpy but benign. Jack is a journalist: sceptical, articulate, dishevelled, according to the screenwriter's model. To these 'conventions', screenwriters Terrel Seltzer and Ellen Simon add that Jack is attractive to women, but afraid of commitment. Melanie is a career woman and single parent: dedicated, hardworking, a perfectionist, wary of men. When they first meet, Melanie characterizes Jack as 'totally ex-husband' in his actions and slovenly manner. Arguably, the rest of the film is concerned with his attempt to overcome this image and be seen by Melanie as a responsible adult.

Meanwhile, Jack sees Melanie as full of 'totally ex-wife' attitude. So equally the rest of the film is concerned with her attempt to overcome this image and be seen as a normal limited individual rather than Superwoman. *One Fine Day*'s realism is predicated on the project of showing how the ups and downs of everyday life as portrayed in the film complicate the conventional Hollywood stereotype with which the film began. For example, Jack will discover that Melanie is devoted to her son and 'inside, she's mush'. The characters of Melanie and Jack are also distinguished by the particular names chosen for them. These make them seem to be particular types of people with particular stable identities – real individuals with real identities such as you and I have.

Other characters are little more than Hollywood occupational traits. Lew is crusty but kindly. Mr Leland is Melanie's crusty but benign boss. Jack's daughter, Maggie, is sweet-natured, loves cats and wanders a lot. Sammy is appealing, but a handful. Celia the journalist is sexy, but hard as nails. Like many a Hollywood-style New York cop before him, Officer Bonomo is gruff but kind-hearted, and of Italian extraction. The realism comes in the way in which the more complex, realistic characters Melanie and Jack interact with them, the peripheral characters seeming to provide a feasible background from which Melanie and Jack spring. Meanwhile, following Melanie and Jack's progress, we identify with the lead characters. They become us.

### Causal connections

In Hollywood narratives, causal connections are tied into how characters act in the situations in which they find themselves. The connections the narrative establishes must be motivated by what we know about the characters and the plotted events.

- Melanie and Jack must liaise with one another throughout the day because they have inadvertently swapped their mobile phones.
- As a result, Melanie receives calls from Lew and Celia, while Jack receives calls from Rita.
- Gradually, as Melanie and Jack decide to forget their initial hostility and cooperate, they not only learn more about and come to like each other, but also their contact with the

▶ Consider the physical characteristics of the peripheral characters in *One Fine Day*. Do these characteristics make them more real? ●

From top to bottom: *Lew the Editor/Bonomo the Cop/ Mr Leland the Architect*

▶ Does it make any difference to these scenes if you turn the sound off? ●

▶ So Leonardo is not part of the New York skyline … Why should this be significant to you if you live in Leonardo? Where is *One Fine Day* set? What effect does this film's setting have on the film itself and your reaction to it? Compare the two settings and the importance of each one to each film. ●

other characters increasingly implicates them in each other's lives.

- While searching for Elaine Lieberman, whom he needs to substantiate an exposé he is writing, Jack runs into Rita, who enjoys reading his column and finds him attractive, at Elizabeth Arden's Red Door Spa on Fifth Avenue, where Mrs Lieberman is enjoying treatment.
- Melanie, who has inadvertently mislaid Maggie, decides to go to City Hall where Celia has told her Jack will be at a 4 p.m. press conference with Mrs Lieberman.
- On Jack's way there, Officer Bonomo tells him that Maggie has been found and, confused, Jack goes and picks her up.
- At the conference he meets a relieved Melanie, who has been haphazardly covering for him in his absence.
- Melanie and Jack share Jack's glory as he exposes the mayor for receiving illegal campaign contributions.
- Finally, smitten with Melanie, Jack insists that he and Maggie replace Sammy's class goldfish, earlier eaten by Lew's cat.

Each move in this scenario leads on from the last and in turn sets up the next, each step reinforcing our sense that Melanie and Jack will end up together.

## Clerks

*'That's what life is. A series of down endings.'*

Both *One Fine Day* and *Clerks* observe realist narrative principles; however, *One Fine Day* has a happy ending in which all issues are resolved, while *Clerks* has an open-ended conclusion. If *One Fine Day* hurtles through a single day measured in hours and minutes, *Clerks* consists of a series of scenes that are apparently plotless.

Appearing in 1993, *Clerks* represents a key moment in the emergence of the US indie film. Attempting to push at the boundaries of what American films could represent, the American independents of the 1980s and 1990s continued a 'post-classical' (roughly post-1960s) project designed to review and revise the look and feel of American cinema. Written and directed by first-time director Kevin Smith, on a tiny budget of $27,000 and using non-actors, *Clerks* is set in the unremarkable milieu of suburban Leonardo, New Jersey (an actual place overlooking the famed New York skyline, but, significantly, not part of it). Along with such films as *Slacker* and *Dazed and Confused* (Richard Linklater, 1991 and 1993), *Clerks* was seen to reintroduce the genuine experiences of young Americans through the rambling conversations of Dante and his friend Randal, who, respectively, man the tills in a convenience store and a video store.

## Editing

Unlike a mainstream project in which right of 'final cut' is a jealously guarded privilege granted only to big-name directors, *Clerks* was edited by Kevin Smith himself. The film consists of a series of thematically defined scenes announced by subtitles: 'Vilification', 'Malaise', 'Harbinger', 'Lamentation', 'Catharsis' etc. These scenes are shot in 90-degree, or eye-level, camera set-ups, and thus present characters as if we are placed nearby to observe and hear what is going on. There is no shot/reverse-shot cutting within scenes, as exchanges are shot in simple two-shots. In fact, Smith seems to mock the shot/reverse-shot format in the scene in which Dante and Randal drive to their friend's funeral. Observing their conversations from the back seat, the camera swings from speaker to speaker even though only the back of his head can be seen. This tends to draw our attention to the camera, a tendency discouraged in Hollywood editing practice.

When Dante and his old flame Caitlin meet in the store, shots of Jay and Silent Bob outside the video store are inserted, making them seem like a chorus commenting on the main action. Staged in mid shot and in low key light, these shots are more deliberately stylized than those of Dante's day, reinforcing our sense that they are meant to stand out from the rest of the film.

Silent Bob supplies the ghetto blaster and Jay starts dancing to a thrash metal track. Used as a kind of punctuation, contrast this with the scene in *One Fine Day* in which Melanie, Jack and the children dash through the park to a rock song on the soundtrack. In *Clerks* the music emerges out of the action of the film. In *One Fine Day*, the music comes as an accompaniment out of nowhere. Shot with a stationary camera, Dante and Caitlin's bickering does remind you of the bickering would-be couples of Hollywood romantic comedies. As Dante and Randal complain about

▶ When we hear a joke, the way it is told tells us how to enjoy it. The way a film sets up a situation is no different. Because the funny incidents in *Clerks* appear to take place in everyday surroundings they seem more like life and less like jokes. So does thinking about the strategies used to make *Clerks* seem real make it less real, less funny? ●

▶ 'Quirky' and 'gritty' are often used by critics to talk about realist film-making. But what do these words actually mean? ●

their customers, there is a series of inserted vignettes of their worst daily bugbears. In the credits these characters are described as: Tabloid Reading Customer, Leaning Against Wall, Milk Maid, and so on. Such labelling defines them according to how these characters are seen and, as this is all Dante and Randal know of these characters, they become for us, too, like strangers glimpsed in public, defined only by what we see them doing. Beyond this, they serve no narrative purpose. There are also inserted shots from around the store – a spinner ad for fruit pies and a surveillance mirror – that also punctuate the action. Throughout the scenes in the store, you are like a customer witnessing interactions going on around you. The film was even shot in black-and-white to emulate the kind of surveillance camera footage taken in stores such as this. Yet the intertitles and 'commentary' from Jay and Silent Bob definitely suggest that you experience it in a particular way.

### Characterization

Like other US independent films which appeared in the 1990s, *Clerks* contains characterizations which were seen to be more realistic, more 'quirky', than polished Hollywood characterizations.

If you grew up in a small town in the 1990s, it is not difficult to see yourself and your friends in these characters. Inhabiting a community with few opportunities to realize their potential, these characters are bored and uninspired. But if *Clerks* appears at first to be a sequence of random events and conversations, a formless narrative apparently lifelike, you will be surprised at how it changes on subsequent viewing. In fact, revolving increasingly around Dante's uncertain romantic and vocational prospects, it comes to seem more and more like a conventional romantic comedy. On the other hand, Dante only *decides* to make up with his girlfriend, so that the film remains open-ended. And for all his tribulations, does he really gain self-knowledge? *Clerks'* ambiguity means the film can be read either as conventional or as realistic.

Veronica and Caitlin may seem like friends of yours, but in key respects they resemble stock Hollywood characterizations. Falling roughly into the conventional nice girl/*femme fatale* moulds, Veronica and Caitlin are defined by a male view:

*Caitlin, the modern femme fatale (top); her older sister: Joan Bennett in* Scarlet Street

Dante's. Veronica is his long-term girlfriend. She is kind, caring and dependable – 'low maintenance', in his words. Caitlin, by comparison, is beautiful, sexy, independent and worldly. Dante wants her rather than Veronica. While we are introduced to Veronica from the outset, Caitlin receives a big build-up, arriving from out of town after Randal spots an announcement of her engagement. Consider how Caitlin's appearance is announced. Dante looks off-screen and there is a huge burst of strings on the soundtrack. We then cut to inside the video store where Randal is looking for a movie. This has the effect of delaying Caitlin's entrance, and tends to associate her with the world of movies.

If Veronica is prosaic, Caitlin is mythologized. The *femme fatale* is a staple character in film noir, a strand of Hollywood thriller that emerged in the 1940s. Like Caitlin, the *femme*

▶ Is Dante and Caitlin's progress from animosity to affection in one scene a parody of the Hollywood model? Or is this how real couples behave? ●

*fatale* is glamorous and mysterious, and as a generic archetype she responds to male insecurities. As with the Hollywood couple, *Clerks* wants you to think that love is a bickering couple. Like Melanie and Jack, who bicker throughout the film, and will, we are supposed to think, bicker into married bliss, Dante and Caitlin have a long argument before agreeing to a date, while Dante and Veronica do nothing but argue.

Yet, for all their apparent conventionality, neither Veronica nor Caitlin quite fits the Hollywood archetypes. The script introduces contradictory qualities to both characters. For all Veronica's 'low maintenance', it is Caitlin who returns to Leonardo to be with her old boyfriend. While the doting Veronica leaves Dante, Caitlin ends up traumatized by a sexual encounter in the store toilet. As with Melanie and Jack, motivated partly by scripted character and partly by plotted incident, it is easy to appreciate that Veronica and Caitlin conform to the Hollywood model of realistic characterization.

A conversational thread running through *Clerks* finds Dante and Randal arguing about *The Return of the Jedi* (Richard Marquand, 1983). Their conversation concerns the small contractors working on the *Death Star* who would have been killed when it was destroyed. Again, *Clerks'* parody of mainstream Hollywood comes into focus. Parody is a humorous, exaggerated imitation of a style, in this case Hollywood cinema. Indeed, two very minor players in a US indie film discussing very minor players on a big-budget film could be seen as a clever commentary on the status of the US indie movie as a place where minor players – small fry – limber up for bigger things. Smith actually had actors play more than one role, effectively mocking the traditional Hollywood identification between star and role. The characters' conversation also finds these small-towners mocking Hollywood.

*Playing on its 'alternative' countercultural image, the publicity tagline for* Clerks *ran: 'A Hilarious Look at the Over-the-Counter Culture'.*

Descended from a long line of best buddies in Hollywood comedies going back to Laurel and Hardy in the 1930s, Randal and Dante fight constantly, but are reconciled in the end. Perhaps *Clerks* is really about their friendship, rather than Dante's love life. In this comedy of character, it is Randal's pranks – disrupting the funeral, selling cigarettes to minors, meddling in Dante's affairs – which motivate the plot. And it is Randal's chatter that keeps us listening.

Like the peripheral characters in *One Fine Day*, the other characters in *Clerks* are each sketched with a single characteristic. Jay and Silent Bob are inseparable. Jay is a shoplifter and constantly searches for sex and drugs. Silent Bob seems to keep their money and has one speech, a word of wisdom to Dante on the subject of women. It recalls Melanie's 'Author's Message' at her drinks appointment at 21 with her boss's clients in which she offers them (and us) her insight into the problems of pursuing a career at the same time as raising children.

*'There are many fine-looking women in the world. They don't all bring you lasagne at work. Most of them cheat on you.' Silent Bob*

## Causal connections

*'I'm not even supposed to be here today.'*

If some of its connections seem unlikely, *Clerks* relies upon whimsical events to generate a sense of lifelike realism. The narrative is (apparently) a rambling mishmash of minor incidents and conversations. Yet it has some astute plotting. Indeed, Smith cleverly sets each of Dante's degradations up with believable ease. He wants you to believe in his plotting precisely because it is more quirky and strange than the perfect engineering of a Hollywood plot. When *The Return of the Jedi* first appeared audiences rioted because the plot was too confusing. The reference in *Clerks* mocks the pretensions of the mainstream. *Clerks* consists of funny little events because life often consists of funny little events. After all, this is the appeal of many jokes we tell each other.

- A customer regales other customers on the hazards of smoking.
- Randal tells Dante that his old girlfriend Caitlin is getting married.
- A hockey game is played on the store roof, but abandoned after ten minutes when the ball is lost.
- An old man asks Dante for a magazine, then goes to the toilet.
- Hearing that one of their school friends has died, Dante and Randal go to the wake, but then have to leave when Randal knocks the casket over.
- A trading inspector fines Dante for selling cigarettes to minors.
- Caitlin shows up, declaring that she has broken off her engagement and wants to date Dante again.

- The anti-smoking guy is discovered to be a chewing gum salesman.
- When Caitlin goes to the toilet she is traumatized by the old man.
- Caitlin goes into shock and is taken to hospital.
- Randal has told Veronica about Caitlin, and she is upset.

## The sound

Both *Clerks* and *One Fine Day* use songs to take a breather, as it were, with the songs forming interludes in the action. In *One Fine Day* a song is used to make a kind of plateau in the character's progress. For example, after Melanie finds out from Maggie that Jack is not dating Celia, there is a scene in which adults and children dash through the puddles in Central Park to the triumphant strains of Tina Arena's 'Love's Funny That Way'. Earlier, as Melanie gazes out of the cab window at the Circle Line boat, there is a reprise of Natalie Merchant singing 'One Fine Day', a song containing a line about 'love that was meant to be'. Along with the river Melanie sees, the song reinforces the sense we get of this love story's natural flow. In turn this naturalizes the possibility that in the real world this happens. When Melanie dresses and puts on make-up to meet Jack at the end, the scene is cut to the Chiffons' version of 'One Fine Day'. At these moments the narrative seems to stop to make way for a kind of celebration of romantic love as in an opera. Music is often used to accompany Melanie and Jack's activities. When they create superhero costumes for Maggie and Sammy, the Shirelles sing 'Mama Said':

> *Mama said they'd be days like this,*
> *Days like this, my Mama said …*

We watch this scene unfold in a series of 'before' and 'after' cuts, as the children are prepared to the rhythm of the song. While the plot motivates the scene, the music not only provides a commentary on this trying day, but also structures the scene. While Melanie tries to awaken the sleeping Jack at the end, Maggie and Sammy watch *The Wizard of Oz* (Victor Fleming, 1939) in Sammy's bedroom. It is an apt choice because in this musical the real turns into dream and dreams become what is apparently real, just as in *One Fine Day* love puts realism to music.

▶ While music often helps to form the narrative of a film, there are also times when it does not perform this function. Think about what music in movies does for you. Does it have to tell a story, or can it interact with the film in some other way? ●

One Fine Day: *music in the air (top)*; Clerks: *the sounds of everyday life*

At one point in *Clerks* Olaf the Russian metalhead breaks into song with his latest tune 'Berserker', integrating this song into the narrative. Like the radio 'soundtrack' which often accompanies manual workers in real life, music in *Clerks* tends to run freely throughout the film. 'Can't Even Tell' was written especially for the film, its very title suggesting the open-endedness and unpredictability of Dante's day.

## Soundtracks

Since 1927 the evolution of Hollywood sound technology has sought to re-create a realistic 'soundscape', yet has tended to put dialogue first. In October 1927 sound sequences were added to the silent film *The Jazz Singer* (Alan Crosland). Regarded as the first 'talkie', it revolutionized film art. Although its sound sequences were for musical numbers rather than dialogue, it was in the advent of voices on screen that the new technology was seen to bring realism to character and narrative. The 1930s saw the emergence of the 'backstage musical' with its combination of songs and realistic chatter. The era also saw the rise of the fast-talking 'screwball comedy' revolving around romantic plots and driven by witty dialogue for its day, this genre being the forerunner of *One Fine Day*.

Debate during the early sound period turned upon whether the soundtrack should reproduce a realistic soundscape of incidental noises – traffic, birdsong, rain – as well as dialogue and music. Or whether it should reproduce only voices. It was decided to opt for a single microphone placed in such a way as to emphasize the dialogue. This technical decision helped Hollywood films serve the needs of narrative rather than a lifelike realism full of contingent everyday sounds.

Until the late 1940s, sound was recorded on set using bulky and noisy electromechanical equipment. The development of magnetic tape after World War II meant smaller, lightweight transistorized recording devices that produced a better signal and enabled films to be shot on location. However, because they must be recorded separately, magnetic soundtracks are rarely used in cinemas where the traditional optical soundtrack that runs alongside the image track is still favoured. But optical soundtrack technology has been catching up. Variable-density and variable-hue soundtracks

*The optical soundtrack is the final photographed soundtrack made from a magnetic master track and ready to be combined with the picture on a composite image and sound print. A variable-density, or variable-hue, soundtrack comprises separate striations of varying density across the track's width. The spacing between striations reflects the frequency of the sound recorded, while their density reflects the volume of the sound.*

▶ Is *One Fine Day* a better movie because the sound is better than the sound in early talkies such as *The Cocoanuts*? ●

▶ Do you think this showcasing of what modern soundtracks can do makes a movie more realistic, or can this precision hinder your attention to the narrative? ●

have made for a richer tonal spectrum. In the 1950s stereophonic sound accompanied new widescreen processes, and in the 1960s quadraphonic sound increased the number of speakers, immersing the audience in a film's soundscape. In the 1970s the Dolby system reduced background noise and enhanced the signal so as to create a cleaner sound. In the early 1980s, the development of the THX format saw the emergence of an even cleaner sound that seems to the spectator to be directed straight at them, an effect not unlike the personal stereo. Since 1993, DTS (digital theatre systems) have used soundtrack on CD.

Recent years have seen a return to increased ambient noise on the soundtrack, but now there is much more distinction between noise, voices and music. If you see an early talkie such as the Marx Brothers comedy *The Cocoanuts* (Joseph Santley & Robert Florey, 1929), and compare it with a modern comedy such as *One Fine Day*, the difference in sound texture and quality is astonishing. One is a cacophony, while the other is layered and precise. 'Virtual reality' sound now generates the sensation of sound being environmental, rather than two flat walls of noise projected from speakers either side of the screen. New technology now enables engineers to simulate sound for particular spaces – rooms, car interiors, parks – and particular textures – whispers, gunfire, echoes – as well as localizing sound. Have you noticed how some soundtracks are so distinctive they make you look around the cinema in search of where a noise came from? Indeed, a key reason for the development of the multiplex auditorium was the showcasing of sound technology.

Soundtracks participate in the creation of particular reality effects in a variety of ways, according to the aims of the film. For example, the slashing sound which accompanies the killer's handiwork in the *Scream* films (Wes Craven, 1996/97) tends to underline the key attraction of this 'slasher' strain of the horror film. That strange clacking noise in the woods in *The Blair Witch Project* (Daniel Myrick & Eduardo Sanchez, 1998) could be an animal, the wind disturbing the branches, or something more sinister. Foregrounded in key scenes, the sound exemplifies the way in which a diegetic sound (sound emerging out of the space and time of the film) can cross a line between realism and fantasy. To underline its realism, Spielberg had a whizzing sound followed by a thud as bullets flew through the air and hit soldiers in *Saving Private Ryan* to emphasize that this is how real bullets sound. In 1995 a group of Danish directors drafted a film-making manifesto – Dogme 95 – as a 'back-to-basics' initiative designed to accompany a fresh approach to cinema. One of its conditions stipulated that sound must accompany the image occurring diegetically. This included music. In the arthouse film, silence can often complement rather than detract from the effect sought. Woody Allen's *Stardust Memories* (1980) is an interesting example because its story of a film director experiencing a crisis of confidence actually enables the film to reflect upon arthouse aesthetics. Remembering his mother, we see a silent image of mother and son indulging his love of magic. The scene works because we tend to remember without sound. In television, we tend to associate canned audience laughter with situation comedies such as *Friends*, while the genuine laughter of a studio audience is associated with stand-up comedy such as Graham Norton or political debate shows such as *Question Time.*

## New technologies

Recent developments in new technologies have also brought about a greater impression of immersion in a film's narrative. If the traditional spectator sat in a cinema darkened so as to generate the illusion that it was just them and the film, maximizing their involvement, a virtual reality (VR) headset will now surround the wearer in the sensory consequences of what seems a whole other real world.

Computer-generated images (CGI) have been around since the 1970s. *Alien* (Ridley Scott, 1979) used CGI to simulate the control panels in the galactic mineral freighter *Nostromo*. In 1982 *Tron* (Steven Lisberger) went a little further by using CGI to generate an entire world as electronic and binary as that inside a computer. Early experiments sought to emulate and celebrate the coming of the cybernetic environment in which we now live. CGI has since been used to generate everyday worlds from the child's nursery of *Toy Story* (John Lasseter, 1995) to the image photo-compositing through which Tom Hanks interacts with President Lyndon Johnson in *Forrest Gump* (Robert Zemeckis, 1994). In 1993 *Jurassic Park* (Steven Spielberg) combined CGI dinosaurs with Go-Motion software, rendering the dinosaurs more

*A scene from* Toy Story

Jurassic Park's *CGI dinosaurs escape. It is as if Spielberg is asking, 'What if CGI invaded every film we saw?'*

► Does it matter that these films bear much less material resemblance to what is being represented than even Méliès' *A Trip to the Moon* (1902)? How many of your favourite films were made using image manipulation? ●

► Is the old-style movie and its unique way of seeing real space and real time becoming a museum piece? Why or why not? ●

realistic with live-action footage to make the illusion of a prehistoric theme park transparent. In 1999 *The Matrix* (Andy & Larry Wachowski) found Keanu Reeves's Neo reconstituted as a pre-programmed digital figure in cyberspace. In *The Mask* (David Russell, 1994) CGI worked wonders exaggerating Jim Carrey's facial features, heralding a new era in digital manipulation of familiar actors. In 2001 *Waking Life* (Richard Linklater) was shot on digital video, then manipulated using specially conceived software to combine the fluidity of live-action footage with the bold graphic look of animation. Taking as its subject a character's uncertainty about what is real and what is being dreamt, the form of *Waking Life* constantly disturbs our complacency about the image. James Cameron, director of *Titanic*, has notoriously joked that he would like to make a film using not real actors but their CGI likeness. Playing on Cameron's idea, Richard Linklater has re-created actors Julie Delpy and Ethan Hawke having a conversation about reincarnation.

The IMAX cinema experience immerses the spectator in a wraparound image of such size that you must turn your head to follow the action. VR means that the spectator, or the 'experiencer', interacts with a computerized fictional world via a visor on which three-dimensional graphic images are seen, while stereo sound is heard via headphones. As the person turns his or her head, the computer can pick up the headset's altering spatial relationship to the computer via sensors in the helmet. Data gloves with sensors enable the user to 'manipulate' virtual objects within the cybernetic world. Interactive films available on CD-Rom enable you to pick and mix images and sounds from a database, determining narrative structure, character construction, space and time for yourself.

The evolution of CGI, VR and interactive films has made for a cinema (if it can still be called that) of hyper, or ultra-real, spectacle. Such 'impact aesthetics' help to differentiate these modes from television. But in the 1990s it was widely felt among audiences, critics and academics that the emphasis on special effects had led to the 'dumbing down' of films where narrative and characterization were sacrificed in favour of spectacle. And what of realism? *O Brother Where Art Thou?* (Joel Coen, 2000) re-created scenes of a Southern chain gang on a computer. Emulating a range of past movies set in this milieu, these scenes are very convincing. Yet while prison movies which the film evokes such as *I Am a Fugitive from a Chain Gang* (Mervyn LeRoy, 1932) and *Cool Hand Luke* (Stuart Rosenberg, 1967) were shot in real space and time, CGI manipulates the image down to the last detail. For example, when we see the characters played by George Clooney, John Turturro and Tim Blake Nelson escape from the prison farm, the field of maize amid which we see their heads intermittently bobbing is a computer-generated one combined with the actors' skilful placement.

This takes the image one step further than *One Fine Day*'s 'any day'. Here the image is completely divorced from history, even while persuading you to participate in a story unfolding in an apparently real place: the Deep South of America. Many would prefer movies to be more real rather than for new technologies to become cleverer at simulating the real. The Dogme directors are the latest movement to advocate a naturalistic cinema that is not so dependent upon technology. They insisted upon shooting on real locations using hand-held cameras, and no special lighting or optical work was allowed. The format had to be 35mm academy ratio, as opposed to widescreen format.

## The realist scale

A realist sliding scale (see diagram on p. 32) might range from fantasy that has the appearance of reality, to reality that has the appearance of representation. At one end of the scale, the BBC documentaries *Walking with Dinosaurs* (1999) and *Walking with Beasts* (2000) used CGI to show what life on Earth was like during and after prehistoric times. At the other end, avant-garde films such as *Meshes of the Afternoon* (Maya Deren, 1943) re-create subjective experience or draw attention to the means by which experience is re-created in mainstream films. Such a spectrum might begin at one end with the artificial representation of the real, proceed through ever more existing realities, until we arrive at *Empire* (Andy Warhol, 1964), a static, single-shot record of New York's Empire State Building during the course of a single day. The spectrum then moves through films that become increasingly stylized and preoccupied with foregrounding their methods of representation. Somewhere in between is experience caught as if unawares.

▶ Is it not paradoxical that while Hollywood strives to re-create the sensory dimensions of experience, some prefer downscale movements such as Dogme because they are more 'real'? Do you think this makes sense? ●

*A possible realist scale*

*Pleasantville* (Gary Ross, 1998) is an amusing exploration of the depiction of experience in films and TV programmes. In it David and his sister Jennifer find themselves magically transported into the world of a 1950s TV show. When they were watching it, it was just a creaky old TV show. When they are in it, the show becomes their world and our 'world'.

▶ Compare the way in which *Pleasantville* the movie began with the way in which David and Jennifer's excursion begins. ●

▶ How and why is it possible to enjoy these counter cinemas because they are different from the norm? Recognizing difference is a big step towards asking yourself why some films are different. ●

## Hiding the apparatus/foregrounding the medium

The most amazing thing about Hollywood films is the way in which they simultaneously suck you in yet still hide the means by which they do so. Hollywood narratives need to be transparent. They have to give the impression that they are a window through which you see the real world so that you can get on and follow the story. This means that narration in a Hollywood film must be motivated by what goes on in this world. In *One Fine Day* we find an apparently gratuitous 'artistic' narrational device in the split screen; however, given the film's emphasis upon grounding characters in space and time, and in their conversations, this device avoids the problem of having voices emanating apparently from nowhere. In the Hollywood film what really counts is being wrapped up in the 'reality' of the film.

However, there are traditions of film-making that deliberately draw attention to the *way in which action unfolds*. They do so in order to expose the ways in which Hollywood and its imitators operate. We saw how an 'alternative' film-making practice can 'parody' mainstream Hollywood when we examined *Clerks*. Because other film-making practices use strategies that interfere with easy identification and involvement, these effects cause 'distanciation' of the spectator. Distanciation devices tend to serve a political purpose, so we associate them with avant-garde or 'counter' cinemas. On a visual level, rapid cutting, unmatched shots and jump cuts have the effect of disorientating you. Unmotivated subtitles, characters speaking directly to camera and non-diegetic inserts have the same distancing purpose. Like a political lecture, Jean-Luc Godard's work in the 1960s was narrated straight to the audience in the form of written or spoken statements and slogans. In *Une Femme est une femme* (1961) a couple argue, but before doing so they turn and bow to the audience. On the narrative level, 'overloading' or 'underfilling' the film makes it seem self-conscious, making you think about how mainstream narratives bear meaning. In *Zabriskie Point* (Michelangelo Antonioni, 1970), for example, we see a building explode over and over again, each time from a different perspective, debris tumbling through the air in slow motion. It comes to appear quite beautiful. But what does it mean? Does every image of a film have to contribute to the narrative or mean anything? On the level of characterization, a character's anonymity, two-dimensionality or inscrutable looks can also distance you from identification. *L'Humanité* (Bruno Dumont, 1999) features a hero whose appearance and behaviour seem so mysterious as to disrupt our involvement in the film.

Led by Godard, the French New Wave directors of the 1960s used devices ranging from jump cuts to direct address to challenge mainstream film-making, and to celebrate cinema itself. A time of widespread political unrest, the 1960s saw the emergence of counter cinemas from British director Ken Loach to the US indie forerunner Direct Cinema and the 'oppositional' docudrama *The Battle of Algiers* (Gillo Pontecorvo, 1966). Heavily influencing the revolutionary practices of the 1960s was the work of playwright Bertolt Brecht. Distanciation derives from Brecht's theory of 'alienation'. By distancing the audience from traditional involvement in the drama, a play or film alienates the audience from the values it represents, a position from which it can criticize those values. By showing how ideology and institutions operate, Brecht sought to show how they could be changed. In his own theatrical productions Brecht would interrupt the action to show what might have happened, indicating how predetermined mainstream character causality is. Some Brecht plays even used projected titles predicting the outcome of a scene.

In the Soviet cinema of the 1920s alienation lay behind editing strategies which tried to show Russian audiences how cinematic images work, a project which assisted their political education following the 1917 Communist Revolution. Using powerful and symbolic juxtapositions of shots, the work of theorist/film-makers Lev Kuleshov and Sergei Eisenstein

*Woody Allen's parody* Stardust Memories *contains an example of 'overloading' in which a couple have just seen an art film and one says to the other: 'What do you think the significance of the Rolls-Royce was?', to which her companion replies: 'I think that's … uh, uh, represents his car.'*

reinvented the cinema as a powerful political tool, indirectly demonstrating the subtle workings of Hollywood and other mainstream cinemas and laying the groundwork for all political film-making to come.

Continuity errors inadvertently draw the spectator's attention to the contrived nature of a film or TV programme. If a character wearing a dark green sweater in a room crosses into another room, at which point there is a cut, then they are seen wearing a light green sweater, we tend to notice. If the weather as seen from indoors is bad, but is sunny in the next shot as we look in from outdoors, we tend to notice. Continuity errors can be fun to spot. They can even be part of why we watch. Director Edward D. Wood Jr made films so full of continuity gaffes that his work is renowned for its ineptitude, drawing a cult audience encouraged by Tim Burton's celebratory *Ed Wood* (1994).

# 3. Genre and Audience

*Here we examine how differing genres shape real experience with reference to genre as a social ritual. How do genres interact with each other over the issue of real experience? How does genre operate in the US independent film? The final part of the chapter offers an overview of the interaction between film and audience in shaping the realism of mainstream and independent films. Questions will be asked about how genres and stars shape our expectations of realist cinema.*

Genre provides an interesting and very important key to our understanding and appreciation of the way films shape experience. Its role is twofold. Traditionally, genre figures prominently in the marketing of new films. For example, the poster for *One Fine Day* shows Melanie in Jack's arms, promising laughs and romance in equal measure, while the stars are shot in high key light, standard practice for the comedy genre. Trailers, too, set up generic expectations. Notice how trailers for horror films such as *Scream* (Wes Craven, 1996) rely heavily upon shock editing, echoing the shocks to come. Marketing devices collude in ideas about genres that are shared by industry and audience. We recognize a particular genre by its characteristics and 'conventions'.

Perhaps the most distinctive genre is the Western. Westerns traditionally feature a battle between clearly defined good and bad men set somewhere in the deserts, plains or mountains of the American West, and are usually set roughly between the end of the American Civil War in 1865 and 1900. They often

*'The nine occupants of Ford's stagecoach neatly represent most of [the iconic characters of the Western genre]: the incorruptible marshal; the comic side-kick; the crooked banker; the whiskey drummer; the gambler; the drunken doctor; the 'good bad girl'; the Eastern lady; and finally the Ringo Kid, the outlaw hero.' (John Saunders, discussing John Ford's film* Stagecoach *(1939), in* The Western Genre: From Lordsburg to Big Whiskey, *pp. 10–11)*

*John Ford once introduced himself with the words: 'I'm John Ford; I make Westerns.' Quoted by Phil Hardy in the* Aurum Film Encyclopedia of the Western, *1995, p. ix.*

take place in frontier towns, featuring characters that have accumulated iconic status over decades of Western film history. Western plots often revolve around the bringing of civilization to the frontier in the form of law, education and culture. Indeed, the characters and conventions of the genre emerged in the 1900s out of the travelling Wild West shows, reproducing a mythicized version of actual Western history which seemed to reinforce the genre's relationship with real experience. Classic Western director John Ford immortalized this era in American history in *My Darling Clementine* (1946). In film writer Bernard Dick's words: 'the frontier is changing: the one-street town of Tombstone (*a real place*, my italics) sports a barber shop where a haircut is capped by a spray of cologne; a church is being dedicated; an actor gives a Shakespeare reading; Clementine (Cathy Downs) becomes Tombstone's first teacher' (*Anatomy of Film*, 1990, p. 89).

There have been more Westerns made in Hollywood than films of any other genre, and the genre has undergone many aesthetic mutations. The Italian spaghetti Western of the 1960s and 1970s pared it down until plots consisted of little more than a horseman riding into town, purging it of wrongdoers, and riding out. The rest was style: fancy gunplay, tense close-ups, Mexican guitars. Celebrating the Western's fascination with gunplay, *The Quick and the Dead* (Sam Raimi, 1995) was an American film which reclaimed the dusty streets and violent minimalism of the Italian films and pushed spaghetti conventions to the brink of parody. Ford's *Stagecoach* (1939) revolves around the journey, an important Western narrative structure in which characters experience physical and emotional hardship and gain self-knowledge. It recurs throughout Western history. *Unforgiven* (Clint Eastwood, 1992) is another example of this journey structure, one which chimes with the nineteenth-century American experience, however stylized the Western has become.

Genres tend to come in and out of fashion. Musicals, a staple Hollywood genre until the 1960s, have experienced a slight revival with *Dancer in the Dark* (Lars von Trier, 2000), *Moulin Rouge!* (Baz Luhrmann, 2001) and *Chicago* (Rob Marshall, 2002). However, such movies as the *Scream* films and the trilogy *American Pie* (Paul Weitz, 1999), *American Pie 2* (James B. Rogers, 2001) and *American Wedding* (Jesse Dylan, 2003) rely heavily upon non-diegetic soundtracks featuring bands whose work these films help to market. The exploitation of the soundtrack is a characteristic of the contemporary Hollywood blockbuster. Aimed at a teen audience, and following the fortunes of a high school teacher in a tough Los Angeles neighbourhood, *Dangerous Minds* (John N. Smith, 1995) plays to a soundtrack featuring Coolio and Wendy and Lisa, a key peripheral in the film's promotion.

## Genre and realism

Genres connect with real experience in another way. Aside from being a marketing tool with which Hollywood films reach a particular audience that thereby recognizes and makes sense of the film, genre is a form of social ritual. Rituals are procedures that have become fixed by repetition. We like the comfort of such rituals as eating dinner, going on a date, or watching genre movies because they offer easy and predictable ways of dealing with essential needs. The pattern of conventions embodied in a particular genre is more than a way in which audiences and critics can identify particular examples. Genre films respond to particular moments in the life of an audience and a society. If genre conventions are comforting because they offer a way into the film, genre movies are comforting because they offer imaginary contexts and solutions in which real questions and issues can be 'resolved', at least for the duration of the film. For example, during the 1950s a number of Westerns appeared in which heroes increasingly took on the characteristics of villains. The *Naked Spur* (Anthony Mann, 1953) is an especially powerful example. Such a preoccupation responded to widespread debate in postwar America about masculine social roles. The Western and the war film provided stages for the imaginary resolution of these issues. In the 1960s the theme of Native American oppression and suffering was emphasized in Westerns, responding to a time of widespread civil rights activism in the United States.

## The romantic comedy

*One Fine Day* belongs to the genre of romantic comedy. What does its genre reveal about *One Fine Day*'s relevance to experience? Again, the genre provides a context in which social tensions can be played out in a harmless way. Traditionally, the romantic comedy is the site of the so-called

*Genres 'reflect the basic questions, problems, anxieties, difficulties, worries and, more generally, the attempt to tackle those basic questions and problems.' (Warren Buckland, Teach Yourself Film Studies, 1998, p. 79)*

▶ Have you ever asked yourself why a particular film appeared at a particular time? Choose a film and research the year in which it was released. What light does this history throw upon the film's themes and preoccupations? ●

► Steve Neale and Frank Krutnik, theorists of the romantic comedy, have argued that in these films the woman must be brought around to the idea of romantic love, according to a patriarchal view of sexual relations. Is this a fair reflection of real relationships between men and women? ●

*Extreme opposites in background, taste and acting techniques, yet both strong-willed and eccentric by Hollywood standards, they formed a most remarkable screen team in nine films.*
Katz on Spencer Tracy and Katharine Hepburn in the *Macmillan International Film Encyclopedia*, 1998, p. 621

► How do similarities between stars and the roles they play have any bearing on how we make sense of films? ●
► What other films can you think of in which a star's role reflected the individual actor in some way? ●

'battle of the sexes' in which issues surrounding the social and sexual roles of men and women are worked through in a witty and poignant way by likeable and attractive stars. We have already noted *One Fine Day*'s stylistic devices that recall romantic comedies of the past. Indeed, the producers evoke the Spencer Tracy–Katharine Hepburn comedies of the 1940s and 1950s as a generic backdrop for their film. These films and *One Fine Day* all fall into a particular variation of the genre known as the 'screwball comedy'.

Emerging in the mid 1930s, the screwball comedy blended the witty and sophisticated dialogue of the maturing talkies with an element of silent comedy 'slapstick', or visual humour. (Think of the man slipping on a banana peel or being hit by a falling bucket of paint beneath a ladder, and you visualize the appeal of slapstick.) In screwball comedy, male characters are typically professionals: professors, reporters or scientists. The term 'screwball' is American slang for an oddball, referring to the fact that one or other of the couple is eccentric or unconventional. Dialogue is brisk, witty and often suggestive. From time to time, chaos breaks out. *The Lady Eve* (Preston Sturges, 1941) finds a clumsy and naive snake expert meeting and falling in love with a confidence trickster after having spent most of his life researching in the Amazon jungle. Critic Bosley Crowther counted six slip-ups at a dinner party, while the scene in which his lover lists her previous lovers is delightfully risqué. In its anarchic way, screwball comedy is quite subversive.

Does any of this sound familiar to you? Melanie and Jack are both high-achieving professionals, their hectic lifestyles driving both a little crazy. Melanie is a determined, intelligent, organized and industrious single working parent. 'Real superwoman! Can't open her door, won't shut her mouth,' according to Jack when they first meet. Jack is a reckless reporter whose sloppy lifestyle and poor timekeeping make him appear, by contrast, incompetent. His apartment is chaotic and has a 'plumbing situation'. Hers is functionally neat. Melanie and Jack spend the entire film bickering and scoring points off each other.

SHE: 'This is a totally ex-husband thing to do.'
HE: 'You would know because that is a totally ex-wife remark.'

SHE: 'Men like you have made me the woman I am.'
HE: 'All the women I know like you make me think all women are like you.'

Doubles entendres – 'thrusting your column in my face' – occur with regularity. That the dialogue is so smart and funny reinforces our sense that these people are meant to get together because they argue so well! Indeed, despite foregrounding gender and the seemingly irreconcilable differences between men and women, the romantic comedy generally appeals to the popular (Hollywood-endorsed) idea that people who bicker together stick together. Losing her cool from time to time, the visual jokes are on oddball Melanie. Dressed in Sammy's dinosaur T-shirt because he spilt fruit juice on her blouse, Melanie climbs on to a cab in desperation at losing track of Maggie. Trying to attain romantic composure for Jack, she backs into a chest of drawers at one point. Melanie's misadventures seem to appeal to some universal idea that sexual frustration manifests itself in clumsy behaviour.

So what does a screwball romantic comedy tell us about contemporary relations between the sexes? Just as they are about to melt into each other's arms, Melanie and Jack confess that they are both afraid of getting emotionally involved. But why should this be? They both find each other attractive. Crucially, Melanie and Jack both like each other's kids. (After initial hostility, Sammy and Maggie get along.) Melanie and Jack seem to work effectively together to achieve their goals.

*One Fine Day*'s relevance has a lot to do with changing patterns in the American labour market. Since World War II, increasing numbers of women have worked to help support their families. Since the 1970s and 1980s, the spread of feminist ideas about a woman's self-determination has fuelled aspirations to pursue careers and to compete with men in professional life. This has changed the nature of marriage, an institution increasingly regarded as a mutual partnership rather than a relationship of dependency. As we know, single-parent women pursue careers nowadays. Notice how a woman of Melanie's mother Rita's generation is bemused by her daughter's 'lifestyle choices' and encourages her and Jack to become a couple. In the film's press pack producer Lynda Obst described the script as an account of the 'gender wars that we've all been living through'.

Produced by Michelle Pfeiffer's production company, *One Fine Day* has less to say to men of Melanie's generation. Jack is a thirty-something male who is frightened of commitment. Meanwhile, much is made of Jack's attractiveness to women. They swoon over George Clooney's dark looks wherever Jack goes! Clooney has become better known for adventure movies such as *Three Kings* (David Russell, 1999) and *Ocean's Eleven* (Steven Soderbergh, 2001) than for romantic comedies, and acknowledges that *One Fine Day* speaks primarily to women. But another feature of the screwball comedy is its promotion of particular personalities. Michelle Pfeiffer made the spoof gangster movie/screwball comedy *Married to the Mob* (Jonathan Demme, 1988) early in her career. Appearing around the same time as *One Fine Day*, the romantic comedy *Multiplicity* (Harold Ramis, 1996) and the thriller *Heat* also worked over issues surrounding the modern couple's attempts to reconcile career and marriage. So generic conventions interact with history and help to create star personas, but how do different generic conventions interact to shape the realism of the Hollywood film?

## Crime films and melodrama

It is important to remember that a genre is never pure. Not only do genres adapt to the concerns of society, but relationships with other genres tend to be slippery, too. Genres are adjacent to one another, so to speak, one genre's outer edges 'imbricated', or overlapping, with the conventions and style of another. One film can be a generically mixed, or 'hybrid', representation of experience. *Heat* displays elements of the family melodrama in its portrayal of cops and gangsters dealing with the domestic fallout from their activities. A crime movie revolving around a bank robber and his gang pulling jobs while pursued by a detective, *Heat* has three subplots involving these men's relationships with wives, girlfriends and a daughter. Diane Venora, Amy Brenneman, Ashley Judd and Natalie Portman got to play a range of scenes in which their characters are rejected, resentful and suicidal, all of which is the stuff of melodrama. Melodramas tend to play out scenes of domestic conflict between family members, featuring strong female characters. In *Heat* key scenes between men and women tend to be well lit, while others are shot low key, signifying the film's status as a film noir, a particular strand of thriller employing low light and harsh angles to communicate a sense of pessimistic dread.

Notice how the charged pursuit of robber by detective is shot at night, focusing attention on the struggle between these men which becomes like a symbolic allegory. An allegory is a story or picture in which the meaning or message is communicated symbolically. Take note also of how stylized the shooting of the climax in *Heat* is, compared with the more prosaic domestic scenes. It helps, of course, when the actors playing the robber and detective are, respectively, Robert De Niro and Al Pacino, who are crime movie icons. Conversely, pure melodramas such as *Moonlight and Valentino* (David Anspaugh, 1995) are shot in high key light. Comedy is also characterized by this kind of 'normal' lighting, as *One Fine Day* shows. The comedy/melodrama *Short Cuts* (Robert Altman, 1993), with its myriad narrative strands and daylit scenes, recalls the high, bright look of TV soap opera. It is often interesting to compare and contrast scenes with similar content in films of differing genres.

There are key scenes in *Heat* and *Short Cuts* that take place in a hospital. In *Heat* the detective Vincent Hanna's teenage daughter Lauren attempts suicide. In *Short Cuts* a little boy, Casey, is in a critical condition after being hit by a car. In *Heat* we are thrown into the scene with close-ups of a distraught mother gabbling incoherently to a nurse. Rapid cuts and fragmented images of nurses, doctors and the patient follow. As the detective calls for a vascular surgeon, he becomes the centre of the scene and the frame, before the focus switches to the doctor taking up the initiative and directing those around him. The editing in *Short Cuts* is more measured, as we see nurses, doctors and Casey's grandfather Paul, who is visiting Casey's parents at the hospital, milling around while Casey's mother, Ann, sits at his bedside. As husband, Howard, joins her, Casey's condition deteriorates. The camera stands by like a sympathetic but helpless observer. When the monitor indicates a crisis in Casey's vital signs, the camera records the growing panic as voices overlap and desperate procedures are put in train. At the end of the scene, the camera calmly observes Paul shuffling off down the corridor. Responding to the soap opera's traditionally conventional record of people

Heat: *In the hospital, the cutting isolates Vincent Hanna and his wife Justine from the doctors and nurses around them, yet we never lose sight of the clinical context with which Vincent interacts to save their daughter.*

*How you respond to coincidences such as Howard's long-lost father showing up in the hospital on the day his son's little boy (Casey) is in intensive care depends on how successful soap operas are as realism.*

interacting, the coverage of the scene in *Short Cuts* acts as a witnessing of the drama and its context, as if we are there as visitors inadvertently seeing all this. It features Paul because Casey's plot strand has been linked to one in which Howard's long-lost father unexpectedly drops in to the hospital to talk to Howard.

Responding to the thriller's traditionally tight plotting and narrative of heroes and villains, the hospital scene in *Heat* rapidly comes to focus on Vincent's taking control. As the focus of the scene shifts from Vincent to the doctor, the camera follows from where the instructions for Lauren's salvation come. In *Short Cuts*, by comparison, we see nurses undertaking emergency procedures which seem (to us) haphazard, before the camera drifts away from Casey. At the end of the scene in *Heat* we are left in no doubt that Lauren will survive. At the end of the scene in *Short Cuts* we, like his parents, must draw the conclusion that Casey did not make it. Both of these scenes are typical of what we associate with melodrama, whether in its 'high' theatrical form as in Shakespeare or here in *Heat*, or in its 'low' everyday form as in soap opera. Thus the way in which *Heat* and *Short Cuts* treat these experiences reveals a great deal about the way genre can shape representation. Consonant with the post-feminist 'work v family' discourse in American life, *Heat*'s and *Short Cuts*' excursions into melodrama demonstrate how generic mutation reflects the historical concerns of audiences.

## Genre films and US independents

As we have seen, US independents often parody mainstream movies and their conventions. *Clerks* is about Dante's love life, although, unlike *One Fine Day*, it is deliberately vague and open-ended on the issue of who will end up with whom. By comparison, we are in no doubt when it comes to *One Fine Day*; fate and everyone else will bring Melanie and Jack together. The tagline for *Clerks* – 'Just because they serve you doesn't mean they like you' – carries no hint of genre. Rather, it suggests *Clerks* is a realistic account of the lot of the convenience store clerk. Compare that tagline with one of the taglines for *One Fine Day* – 'She was having a perfectly bad day ... Then he came along and spoiled it' – which pushes the romantic scenario upfront. Foregrounded in *One Fine Day*, genre plays another role in *Clerks*. Indeed, the looser relationships between Dante, Veronica and Caitlin show how 'different' films such as *Clerks* aim to be and, by implication, how unscripted and lifelike.

Rather than taking genre for granted as Hollywood films do, US independents act as a sort of commentary upon mainstream genres. Indie movies are more likely to be interested in the mechanics of genre, rather than using genre as a means to an end as Hollywood films do. In *The Player* (Robert Altman,

▶ At least that's how Hollywood romantic comedies want you to think. Compare *One Fine Day* with the indie title *Walking and Talking* (Nicole Holofcener, 1996). What do you notice about these films' representations of characters? ●

Theorist Siegfried Kracauer (1889–1966) has written that: 'The cinema ... is not exclusively human. Its subject matter is the infinite flux of visible phenomena – those ever-changing patterns of physical existence whose flow may include human manifestations but need not climax in them.' (Siegfried Kracauer in *Theory of Film*, 1960)

▶ Think about this statement in relation to *Clerks*. ●

1992), a number of jokey comparisons are made between a real murder investigation and a typical Hollywood thriller investigation. While the film turns the real investigation on its head by having the murderer get away with it, the thriller genre is turned on its head by making the hero a murderer. *Passion Fish* (John Sayles, 1992) offers an interesting comparison between the TV soap operas on which millions of us are hooked and arthouse cinema conventions. Seeking to start a new life after an accident, a soap star abandons her career for the uncertainty of life as a lonely paraplegic. Playing the far-fetched scenarios and glamorous life of her career off against a difficult, dull but authentic new life, and employing real locations and an open-ended plot, *Passion Fish* offers a fascinating commentary on mainstream storytelling and another kind of storytelling. So the US independent film performs two distinct functions. It offers realistic alternatives to Hollywood, and it acts as irreverent marginalia, subversive jottings along the edges of mainstream practice.

## Audiences

Given the high costs of film production and the importance of attracting the biggest audiences to a film, it is important that it makes the widest and most universal appeal. A lot of thought goes into marketing a new film so that its audience is effectively reached. Distributors organize tryouts in neighbourhood cinemas in a particular catchment area. Particular films target particular groups and constituencies. *One Fine Day* targeted a middle-class family audience, the day-to-day fare in most multiplexes. *Clerks* targeted students and young people in arthouse cinemas. In order to capitalize on a large local arthouse crowd, multiplexes often have a slot, a 'Manager's Choice', featuring more demanding films for a more discerning audience so as to co-opt the arthouse crowd. Notice how on the *One Fine Day* DVD and VHS the accompanying trailers are also aimed at family audiences.

Have you ever noticed how often trailers for Hollywood films begin with the words: 'In a world in which …'? You then see excerpts of drama, a few close-ups of stars, some violence, some sex, special effects … But not before you have been invited into another world.

Remember, to the executives who 'green light' them and the technicians and crew who make them, films are products

*'… the spectacle of seeing Brad Pitt, Michelle Pfeiffer or Jack Nicholson on screen is a cinematic event in itself and one could be forgiven for thinking that characterisation was only a pretext for bringing this spectacle to the screen.'*
*(Mark Browning, Film and Ideology, Film Education, p. 4)*

of the leisure industry, like CDs, DVDs and theme parks. When you go out and buy a DVD player, you are confronted with a metal box and a list of features. Yet by the time a few weeks have gone by and you are using it regularly, you will have settled into a habitual pattern of usage in which the individual features matter to a greater or lesser degree depending upon how often you use them. Likewise, when you see a film's trailer you are confronted with a series of fleeting contingent effects, a set of impressions. Yet by the time you have seen the film, you will have settled into that 'world in which' each excerpt, each sensation has its place and plays a greater or lesser role in your enjoyment. If by buying a DVD player you have bought into a 'new world of watching', as the ad puts it, a movie is just as much a product which you make use of.

A film's trailer has to promise you a fantasy into which you can escape. But it must also promise you a fantasy in which you can believe. Now what you believe has a lot to do with the kind of film you are watching. For example, you expect to see some pretty crazy stuff when you sit down to watch *Star Wars: Episode II: Attack of the Clones* (George Lucas, 2002). The sci-fi fantasy has a high threshold of believability built into the genre, while a thriller such as *Heat* has a lower threshold beyond which it may not go if it is to take you with it. So however fragmented the attractions of the trailer, you pretty much trust that the drama, the stars, the violence, the sex, the special effects will fit seamlessly into the film when it comes along because that is the kind of trailer you saw. The trailer has set up certain expectations about what kind of film this is going to be. So how does a film such as *One Fine Day* square the attractions of the trailer with the realistic portrayal of contemporary New York working people in such a way as to make you stay seated?

## One Fine Day

Traditionally, Hollywood studios have aimed romantic comedies at women and couples in the twenty-five to thirty-five age range. But each genre film is also different from the genre. This one, like *When Harry Met Sally* (Rob Reiner, 1989) but unlike *Multiplicity*, combines a knowing grasp of psychoanalysis with a 'modern' storyline to appeal to a specific college-educated professional audience. In order to

▶ *One Fine Day* constantly 'finds' Melanie and Jack at particular New York locations. Make a list of them and ask what each location brings to the scene in which it appears. ●

In *One Fine Day*, *Michelle Pfeiffer becomes Melanie Parker, while George Clooney becomes Jack Taylor*

appeal widely, genre movies tend to fall into strands dealing with specific concerns and issues.

We have already seen how Melanie and Jack chime with what we might believe about thirty-something career-orientated single parents today. *One Fine Day* establishes a mutual relationship in an aesthetic sense that echoes the romantic relationship of the plot. What we take to ring true about Melanie and Jack is believable partly because these New York types are seen in their natural habitat, where much of the film was shot. This aesthetic relationship goes both ways, however, in as much as Melanie, Jack and other New York types such as Lew and Officer Bonomo seem to be 'found' amidst *One Fine Day*'s portrait of New York life. We never see these characters outside their working environment: Lew in his office, Bonomo in the police station, for example. The camera 'found' Melanie in her apartment at the beginning. You can see 'You Know Jack' Taylor's face plastered across every other bus in the city.

We have also noted that the main characters have particular names that help to generate specific identities. But look closely at those names: Melanie Parker and Jack Taylor. As it reads on the DVD and video cases: 'In this charming romantic comedy, three-time Academy Award nominee Michelle Pfeiffer (*Dangerous Liaisons*, *The Fabulous Baker Boys*, *Love Field*) and *ER* star George Clooney find that opposites attract whether they like it or not …' On the film's poster, Clooney carries Pfeiffer in his arms in close-up. So what if the stars' and the characters' names are similar? Happy accident? I don't think so. As real as they wanted you to see New York during the evening rush, the producers wanted to make a Michelle Pfeiffer movie.

Obviously, the characters' names do make them seem like particular individuals. But notice how much emphasis is placed upon the stars who play the characters in the publicity. As much emphasis was placed on Pfeiffer and Clooney in the film's trailer. These characters might be distinctive people, real contemporary New York citizens, but isn't their distinctiveness due in large part to the fact that two very distinctive people play Melanie and Jack? The trailer attracts you to see *One Fine Day* because these 'real' characters' lives are brought to you by distinctive and attractive actors, as opposed to people 'found' in that environment as the film suggests. Notice how in the DVD plot synopsis it is the actors, not the characters, who 'find that opposites attract'. The similarity between the characters' and the actors' names, therefore, is no mere coincidence. Like the complementary relationship between the New York types and their New York milieu, the effect is seamless. Star and character will be identified with one another because this product is a 'star vehicle', a project designed to put a star into the limelight and advance their career. Thus they want Michelle Pfeiffer and George Clooney fans out there to go see it. Thus the movie squares its attractions with its realism.

But to pull this assignment off properly, *One Fine Day* had to reconcile its star images with its particular scenario. Before getting this opportunity, George Clooney had become well known for his portrayal of Dr Doug Ross, the emergency-room paediatrician on the TV show *ER*. His last film had been the box office hit *From Dusk till Dawn* (Robert Rodriguez, 1995). Both the TV series and *From Dusk till Dawn* found Clooney playing sympathetically opposite children. *One Fine Day* finds Clooney in sympathetic rapport with young Mae Whitman, who plays Jack's daughter, Maggie. Thus this latest Clooney role would have chimed for British and American audiences with a range of dramatic situations in which the star had already been seen, prompting one Internet Movie Database (IMDb) user to write: 'George Clooney (playing someone rather like though not identical to his *ER* character).'

Michelle Pfeiffer habitually portrays intelligent but emotionally vulnerable young women who embark on risky and uncertain relationships. Her preceding two movies – *Dangerous Minds* and *Up Close and Personal* (Sydney Pollack, 1996) – revolved around characters who value their careers. So the character of Melanie Parker fitted Pfeiffer's image perfectly at this time, as Pfeiffer was also thinking of becoming a mother and her career seems to have been preparing us for the Parker character. It should come as no surprise that Pfeiffer co-executive produced *One Fine Day* for her and Kate Guinzburg's production company, Via Rosa.

When *One Fine Day* appeared it was touted in the press release as 'an old-fashioned love story for the cellular age'. As we know, Hollywood films often foreground new technology, whether in the form of digital graphics which are part of the

Interestingly, in 1996 when *One Fine Day* appeared, mobile phone companies in Britain were beginning to target people in their teens and twenties, and this consumer group has grown and grown since. Since the 1980s, however, public perception of the 'mobile phone user' (if I may coin such a type) was the thirty-something professional. How much did Hollywood films have to do with this perception of real life? Six years later in 2002, the film *Phone Booth* (Joel Schumacher) contained actual statistics on the changed profile of the mobile and its typical user as part of the plot set-up.

film's fabric, as in *The Matrix* (Andy & Larry Wachowski, 1999), or in the shape of actual hardware appearing as part of the scenario. Technology is not something we usually associate with the romantic comedy. But Melanie and Jack's story revolves for much of the film around their mobile phones, prompting another IMDb user to call the film 'A mobile phone fairy tale'. On the other hand, the film relies upon its audience's knowledge of psychoanalysis and good old-fashioned wisdom for its portraits of Melanie and Jack. Melanie accuses Jack of having a 'Peter Pan complex', while Jack accuses Melanie of having a 'Captain Hook complex'. The scene in which Jack uses euphemisms – 'fish', 'cookie', 'cookie-maker' – to his analyst in front of Maggie parodies the tendency in psychoanalysis for words to stand for other things. The fact that Sammy is overly mischievous, while his mother is a control freak, plays with the psychoanalytical cliché that our behaviour is constantly responding to those around us. Celia wants to write an article based upon an old saying: 'Love your guy like a little boy and he'll grow into a man.' I'm sure without thinking too much about this saying, most members of the audience would admit to hearing it somewhere, even if they haven't actually. Traditionally, romantic comedies are aimed at a youngish audience. With its classical editing, older actor Charles Durning as Lew and an old-fashioned ending on the one hand, and George Clooney, a 'modern' couple and distinctive ring tones on the other, *One Fine Day* clearly sought to bring older and younger audiences together in the same multiplex.

Featuring a mixture of romantic 'torch songs' and newer upbeat tracks, the soundtrack to *One Fine Day* makes a broad-based easy-listening appeal to a popular audience which likes its romantic scenarios old-fashioned and bathed in music. Notice how often the action seems to 'stop' while a song plays over a particular, often romantic, scene. From Natalie Merchant's version of 'One Fine Day' and Tina Arena's 'Love's Funny That Way', to the Chiffons' 'One Fine Day', the soundtrack appeals to audience members old enough to remember, or know of, 1960s band the Chiffons, and those to whom Tina Arena and Corrosion of Conformity mean more. Advertised in the credits, the soundtrack was a key sales 'peripheral' in the marketing of *One Fine Day*, as was the published screenplay. A successful film, the film's easy romanticism found an audience of young and old who believe in love and marriage, and trust Hollywood to show it like it is.

## Clerks

The US independent film is usually to be found playing at arthouse cinemas. Although these films tend to riff on the conventions and concerns of mainstream Hollywood cinema, independents also hail from a particular culture and set up expectations of their own. Like the European art film, the indie movie brings with it assumptions about authorship. Like, for example, *Rome, Open City* (Roberto Rossellini, 1945), the indie movie is directed by an individual with his or her own philosophy and own way of communicating it, rather than, as so often in Hollywood, conceived by a committee and produced by a studio. US indie films are often initially showcased at film festivals. Sundance was an important venue for the efflorescence of American independents, out of which *Clerks* appeared. London and Cambridge have a strong US indie section, bringing such work to British attention. Accompanying the release of a US indie film will be interviews with the director in broadsheets and specialist film magazines featuring stories about the making of the film. The marketing of these films tends to emphasize their 'slice-of-life' qualities rather than, as in the marketing of Hollywood films, their exceptional scenarios, their stars or their entertainment or production values. American independent film-making, more like European art cinema, covers a range of titles which do not fall happily into accepted genres. Emphasized here is the individual artistry of these films. The dialogue, the acting, the film's specific sensibility tend to be foregrounded.

The term 'audience' is derived from the Latin verb *audire* (to hear). When you sit down to watch a Hollywood film, not only do you see it, but you hear it, too (a fact which has far-reaching implications, as we shall see in Chapter 4). Consisting of static shots in which characters talk, *Clerks* makes the talky open-endedness of Dante and Randal's lives seem not merely a realistic portrayal of life in this corner of New Jersey, but also cool to an intended audience who revel in its pop cultural references and scatological humour. Look at how the film 'positions' you. As we have seen, when Dante

So we were tempted into the film by the tried-and-tested Michelle Pfeiffer.

▶ Does our recognition of Michelle Pfeiffer add additional meanings to the film? ●

▶ Can we ignore that and get something else out of the film? Would it be the same film? How would it be altered and would you still like it? ●

An important part of what you and other audience members do is get 'unofficial' enjoyment out of a film by misreading or ignoring its official poster appeals. This reading 'against the grain' is something you will doubtless become more and more enchanted by as you study film.

▶ Recall a film that particularly affected you. Write an account of the circumstances, your thoughts and feelings about this experience. Don't leave anything out. ●

▶ Look at three of Kevin Smith's films. See if you can spot any philosophy or recurring themes from film to film. ●

*Dante and Randal, as seen by a friend in the back seat*

and Randal drive to the funeral home, you see them from the back seat, the camera vacillating between Dante and Randal as you follow their conversation. It is as though you are one of their friends sitting in the back for the ride. This camera set-up is part of the film's contract with its 'slacker' audience. Unlike *One Fine Day*'s soundtrack, which consists entirely of love songs, albeit in various styles, here the soundtrack consists of a range of different messages – Violent Mood Swings, Chewbacca, Kill the Sex Player – communicated by different bands. The soundtrack makes an appeal to its audience in its indie musical styles in a way that is thoroughly consistent with the mesh of often subversive voices and perspectives embodied in the film.

# 4. Institutions and Ideology

*In this chapter we look at the roles that social institutions and ideology play in shaping realist representations of experience in films and television, a process in which aesthetics interact with belief systems and the politics that they embody. We will also examine the play of institutions such as governments, politicians, the press, special interest groups, censors, studios and directors in the production of truth and reality effects. We will question the validity of hierarchies of taste and the relationship between representations and real behaviour.*

In Chapter 1 we saw how Hollywood films construct aesthetic effects which strike us as real and true. We saw how such effects naturalize particular experiences and outcomes as if these experiences are inevitably and uniformly linked in real life. As we watch a mainstream Hollywood film such as *One Fine Day*, we are not meant to question its assumptions, but rather just sit back and enjoy their expression.

But the cinema is an ideological institution practised by individuals and groups with a vested interest in the attitudes, values and type of society that their films promote. Aesthetics and experience are seamlessly matched in Hollywood films, such seamlessness enabling Hollywood films to generate ideological messages invisibly, sneaking ideology past us in the guise of entertainment. Taken in by the drive of its narrative and the allure of its surface sheen, it is easy for us to miss, or not bother with, the sense in which *One Fine Day* is promoting a certain way of seeing the world and other people

One Fine Day: Melanie's meeting with business clients at 21, where she cuts the meeting short to be with her son

*I have a child and he has a soccer game in twenty minutes. If he's late he doesn't get the trophy and because I'm in here with you he's probably going to be late. But what gets to me more than anything is that instead of crying about it he's out there with a big old smile pulling fish faces at us. Gentlemen, if you're smart you'll want me as much for my dedication and ability as for the fact that I'm going to ditch you right now and I am going to run like hell across town so that my son knows that what matters to me most is him. And Mr Leland, your real grounds for firing me should be if I should stay here with you.*

Melanie's author's message
One Fine Day

in it. But we must not forget that we *hear* movies as well as see them. Politicians since the dictators Hitler, Stalin and Mussolini in the heyday of mass cinema audiences in the 1930s have realized that films are powerful vehicles for getting messages across. Accustomed to the honeyed drip of Hollywood entertainment, for instance, generations of audiences have also become accustomed to the ideology of this uniquely American cinema.

An ideology is a system of ideas which justifies and underpins a particular economic and political system. A particular country will have a particular ideology upon which its government and institutions are built and which explains not simply their nation's government, but also their whole lives and purposes to the people. Ideologies are put in place by political and social elites to control individuals. In turn, individuals are meant to see themselves in the images and representations that ideologies generate. In a liberal democracy such as Britain, we are told that we are free to live as we please within the law. But this means that each individual is obliged to work every day to make a living and to pay taxes to the government. We also enjoy free speech, but this means that the government I voted for could be voted out by others, and I must put up with the consequences. In another liberal democracy, the United States, individuals enjoy apparent freedoms, but they come with a price.

Films and television programmes are in these societies key communicators of ideology. How do we become aware of the ideological content of the films and television we watch? Well, ideology can be read into a film on either an explicit or an implicit level. The explicit level can be found in a film's publicity. What a producer, star or director has to say about the latest Hollywood release in interview counts as explicit ideological meaning. The producers' comments about how individuals juggle family and career nowadays in connection with *One Fine Day* counts because here is a key player in the film's production discussing the message they hope cinemagoers will take away with them. Distributed at preliminary screenings for the press in the form of 'press packs', these messages often find their way into critics' reviews and 'puff pieces' promoting a film. Melanie's 'author's message', as I call it, finds a character in *One Fine Day* itself discussing the ideology behind its making. In Chapter 2 we saw how particular stars stand for particular values. Melanie/ Pfeiffer's endorsement of working motherhood here can thus be seen as the star image branding the ideological message.

The implicit level on which ideology can be sought is trickier because it involves engaging with the way in which the film generates meaning *as a film*. This is a more interesting level because you have to make a case for a film's reproduction of ideology based upon your own reading of *mise-en-scène*, editing and camerawork. You may argue that the shot/ reverse-shot set-ups between Melanie and Jack near the beginning of *One Fine Day* give way to two-shots as they cooperate more and more, suggesting how working together to achieve their goals brings about job satisfaction and naturally goes hand-in-hand with romantic fulfilment. Such a reading tends to bear out the producers' ideological message. But, as assiduously as Hollywood films promote certain messages about experience, they also repress other messages. You might want to ask tricky questions about *One Fine Day* such as: Are Sammy and Maggie, who disliked each other intensely, going to be happy as stepsiblings? Of course, questions like this seem awfully boring alongside such a harmless and pleasant piece of entertainment. But isn't it precisely because *One Fine Day* is such a guileless entertainment to be drawing us in as it does that such questions are somehow airbrushed out of the picture? While busily promoting the idea that hard-working beautiful people do well and find the right partner, questions about their respective politics and their children's emotional wellbeing are left out. As Rita clearly feels attracted to Jack, how will she deal with her daughter marrying him? Such is the stuff of real experience, not Hollywood romantic comedy.

## 'Miss Johnson, you better be for real.'

*Dangerous Minds* foregrounds ideology much more emphatically than a film such as *One Fine Day,* which, after all, is meant as a diverting star vehicle. In *Dangerous Minds,* high school teacher Louanne Johnson descends from a hallowed Hollywood stereotype that has come to stand for certain values, among them idealism, intelligence and fortitude. If *One Fine Day* contains only one moment in which its ideological project is obviously foregrounded, *Dangerous Minds* is constantly reinforcing its message of

*'For my money, education is the most pressing issue in this country. You can't legislate how people raise their children and the only chance is by reaching them through the schools.' (Michelle Pfeiffer in* Interview *magazine, July 1994)*

Dangerous Minds: *Pfeiffer as teacher*

▶ Why is the high-contrast monochrome scheme associated with music videos associated with realism in *Dangerous Minds'* credit sequence? ●

education equals self-determination. Indeed, this dynamic is built into the film from the moment Michelle Pfeiffer stands in front of her class. Earlier on, we see Louanne studying teaching manuals in an effort to find ways of reaching her disadvantaged students, as if setting a hard-working example to the film's youthful audience. As a teenager, Pfeiffer worked a supermarket checkout. In one scene, Luanne's student Callie is seen efficiently working a checkout. It is easy to imagine the star's influence playing a role in the 'back story' of this smart and, eventually, motivated character.

A reading of the film as a *film* encourages the impression that Louanne 'civilizes' her deprived inner-city charges, offering the chance of another, better life. Not only are their activities – rapping, hanging out, making out – and their discourse – African-American/Hispanic, hip-hop – radically different from that of their 'white bread' teacher, but the distinction is played out on the level of filmic style as well. The credits sequence in which the students are bussed in to school is shot in a high-contrast monochrome scheme often used in pop videos. A vagrant rakes through garbage on the sidewalk. A drug deal is done through an open car window. The opening shot finds a wall covered in graffiti. Here is a world begging reclamation. Only as the buses actually reach Parkmont High does the film change to colour and are individual students singled out. Subsequent scenes charting Louanne's fortunes inside the school are punctuated with shots of the schoolyard full of 'teenage wildlife'. Early scenes find our view of Louanne/Pfeiffer continually blocked by figures passing to and fro in class. Indeed, her first day finds her in a classroom, the *mise-en-scène* of which differs little from the schoolyard. The invisible line traditionally demarcating teacher from student is frequently breached, but as Louanne 'reaches' them, the teacher/star increasingly becomes the focus of their, and our, attention. If the *mise-en-scène* seems initially crowded, the film rapidly learns to create a space for star and spectator, becoming organized into traditional shot/reverse-shot exchanges between Louanne and her students. In the scene in which Emilio and Raul and his confederate fight, atomized, contrasty close-ups of the antagonists predominate. When Louanne arrives, the scene becomes organized around shot/reverse shots that lend the impression that she is healing the rift. It is as though the film is made to toe the line before its prim 'teacher' and the classical style that she represents.

As suffused with ideological assumptions as films are, it is possible to read them 'against the grain', as we came across in Chapter 2. Such readings can produce an interpretation that is at odds with a film's 'official' intentions. For example, do you think that self-determination is the only thing you need to improve your life? The African-American and Hispanic students and their cultures in *Dangerous Minds* seem colourful and dynamic, but how easy is it to buy into the American ideal of individual freedom when your destiny seems to be a spiral of unemployment, poor housing, drug dependence, crime, rehab, prison? One of the most dynamic moments in the film comes after Emilio's girlfriend, Angela, points out to Louanne that Emilio and Raul will fight no matter what, reinforcing the perennial lack of self-determination in these lives. There is then a cut to an energetic locker-room fight in which rapidly cut close-ups of antagonists and spectators fragment the stylistic order that Louanne/Pfeiffer confers elsewhere. Motor-driven by its rock soundtrack, the scene feels like a comic strip. Following such a dynamic scene, can we still remain so convincd by the 'white bread' lessons in self-determination?

'Family values' is central to the ideological ethos of Hollywood films. But what does this term actually mean? Like other discourses such as 'going up in the world' and 'settling down' which drive film after film, 'family values' stands for a series of beliefs and codes of behaviour which Hollywood films naturalize time after time. Notice how Raul is relatively well adjusted because he comes from a stable background with a mother and father. Emilio, by comparison, comes from a broken home. Discourse is an attitude unconsciously embodied in an expression or a certain type of rhetorical language, one designed to impress. We think we know what we mean when we talk about 'family values', but the expression tends to conceal what such values actually are. It also tends to reveal a way of thinking about where values should come from. As we have seen, heterosexual closure is the lot of most Hollywood protagonists.

But in societies in which the divorce rate is high such as in Britain and America, many children share their parents and many parents share their children. What does the term 'family

> *There are a lot of people who live in your neighbourhood who choose not to get on that bus. What do they choose to do? They choose to go out and sell drugs. They choose to go out and kill people. They choose to do a lot of other things. But they choose not to get on that bus. The people who choose to get on that bus – which are you – are the people who are saying: 'I will not carry myself down to die. When I go to my grave, my head will be high.' That is a choice. There are no victims in this classroom!*
> Louanne's author's message
> *Dangerous Minds*

▶ Watch the schoolyard montage in *Dangerous Minds* closely. Do you see how it is the aspects of these people's lives that make them different rather than those that make them like other people that the film focuses on? How is this done? ●

▶ How successful are movies at enabling individuals to work through ethical dilemmas? Is this why we go to the movies? Do you find yourself behaving in certain ways in emulation of characters in movies? ●

values' come to mean in societies such as these? Responding to unhappy upbringings or for other reasons, many people actually prefer being single. What does such a discourse have to say to these people? Is being married and raising a family what everyone needs? Are more children what the world needs? Like 'common sense' and 'knowing right from wrong', such terms are inculcated into us from childhood. Consequently, we never really sit down and think through what they mean. Being 'sensible' and knowing the 'right' thing to do becomes a question of following the particular ethos which prevails in British and American societies, one based loosely upon Christian principles. But as human beings, we each have individual drives and desires, based partly upon individual history and partly upon individual circumstances, which make us act in individual ways. For example, a good many Americans, like a good many Britons, were not brought up to observe Christian principles. The fact is that living in America and Britain obliges individuals to take a particular ideology on board, ideologies put in place to control us.

Living in Britain or America also subjects us to the films and television that those societies generate. This obliges us to view experience in particular ways. But you do not have to accept ideological assumptions unquestioningly. Issue-based Hollywood films such as the AIDS drama *Philadelphia* (Jonathan Demme, 1993) provide sites at which cinemagoers can work through their own thoughts and feelings about these issues. With their familiar characters and day-to-day revelations, TV soap operas such as *EastEnders* and *Brookside*, too, offer a space each evening in which moral issues, usually revolving around families, can be worked through. Yet issue-based drama is as suffused with ideological assumptions as any other genre. Notice how the middle-class lawyer's family in *Philadelphia* accepted his illness without question. Commentators suggested that here the film strained to perpetuate the 'family value' of domestic supportiveness to ameliorate those who considered its tolerance towards gay lifestyles too liberal. In *EastEnders* the sexy, somewhat wayward Kat had an affair with the British West Indian Anthony. Both characters conform to sexist and racist stereotypes of the hot-blooded white woman and the sensual black man which have roots deep in our culture.

## The American Way

Ideas such as the importance of self-determination combined with teamwork, God, family and country underlie the American economy, the American system of government, and the way millions of individual Americans think. For example, in poll after poll Americans have been cited as the most patriotic and most God-fearing of peoples. From the earliest age, American children are taught to become high achievers, while team sports are encouraged in preparation for a corporate economy of punishing targets and team spirit. Embodying many of these values, Hollywood films have always been regarded by Washington politicians as the best advertisements for American ideas and products. For decades, 'product placement', the surreptitious but visible inclusion of consumer items in films and television, has made people around the world aware of the American way of life. We have seen how *One Fine Day* promoted the mobile phone. In 1998 the 'e-mail romance' *You've Got Mail* (Nora Ephron) appeared just as the on-line revolution was gathering pace in Europe, introducing a technology and a jargon which are now common currency. Notice how mobiles and e-mail are taken for granted in these films, not simply clever new technology but integral to the plots, integral to the clever and up-to-date lives that Americans apparently lead.

In the 1910s and 1920s the car, always central to American culture, lent American silent comedy its characteristically frenetic edge, and for the vast numbers of recent immigrants which were the movies' first audiences characterized American society as modern, mechanical and forward-looking. In the 1950s the gadgets of the modern consumer society were showcased in the tail fins, dishwashers and advertising patter of Hollywood comedies and melodramas alike.

Around this time, the teenager first became recognized as a demographic with distinctive cultures. Since the 1960s, assisted by a shift in the average age of audiences, young people have become a key Hollywood target group, the accompanying ideology increasingly geared to promoting a vision of America as a place of young and affluent people free to pursue their dreams. Whole subgenres from the 'slasher horror' film to 'teen movies' such as the *American Pie* films appeared in response to this demographic. Suffused with the ideal of hard work and romantic fulfilment, and furnished

▶ Speaking of jargon, have you ever stopped to wonder where terms such as 'sleepover' and 'makeover' came from? Every minute of every day, we are being Americanized without even realizing it … Do you think this is intentional? ●

with the paraphernalia of an affluent society, such films become sites at which young audiences supposedly work through their ethical dilemmas, their resolutions embodying attitudes which help to socialize individuals to live in western society. Have you ever wondered why *Scream 2* (Wes Craven, 1997) is so preoccupied with the right way to behave? Sydney reveres the slasher's victims. Gale Weathers exploits them. No matter what genre, Hollywood films from *Dangerous Minds* to *Titanic* are vehicles for morality and ideology.

## Meanwhile, back in the real world ...

Yet reality and truth effects distort reality and truth. If aliens watched only Hollywood films and US television, they could be forgiven for thinking that it's a white, male heterosexual world! But in reality women make up more than half the world's population. Black people of a variety of African and Asian descents make up significant proportions of the populations of Britain, Europe and America. Hispanics (Americans of Latin American extraction), Koreans, Chinese and Vietnamese represent growing proportions of American – and British – society. (Spanish even threatens English as the main language in some American cities.) Yet how many Hollywood stars are Hispanic, Korean, Chinese or Vietnamese compared to those that are white? There are African-American actors in the 'A list' of top Hollywood talents. But it was only in 2002 that an African-American woman – Halle Berry – received the Best Actress Oscar at the Academy Awards. There are Hispanic-American actors in the A list – Jennifer Lopez, Benicio del Toro, Salma Hayek – but not many compared with the size of the Hispanic American population. Although there are some women in the A list, a perennial criticism of Hollywood is that there are few women behind the camera. Women produced *One Fine Day*. Yet the director was a man, and many feminists would say that its message was scarcely radical! Famously seen as the emergence of feminist thinking in the mainstream, *Thelma and Louise* (Ridley Scott, 1991) reduced the women's complaint against male-dominated society to a dispute between individuals in true Hollywood fashion. Complaining incoherently about men and leaping off a cliff scarcely changes the world!

How often does a gay or lesbian character head up a Hollywood film as if the presence of gays and lesbians in

*In Chapter 2 I referred to patriarchy in connection with what romantic comedies expect of female characters. Patriarchy is a form of social organization or government in which men rule and power descends through the male line.*

everyday life was the most natural thing in the world? *Philadelphia*, you might reply. But isn't the Hollywood 'issues movie' a case of special pleading on behalf of constituencies that the studios feel they ought to represent now and again? How often does a disabled or dyslexic character head up a Hollywood film as if the presence of disabled or dyslexic people in everyday life was the most natural thing in the world? Given the actual make-up of American society (or any other society), these minorities are poorly represented. This demonstrates how conservative Hollywood's view of the world is because, by implication, if Hollywood excludes balanced representations of these constituencies, they exclude the outlooks and contributions which these constituencies make. While seeking to provide an account of the emergence of today's multi-racial America, *Forrest Gump* (Robert Zemeckis, 1994) repressed the often distressing complexities of American history. Indeed, although the film did revolve around a member of an under-represented group in the backward Forrest Gump, it elicited criticisms that, seen through his eyes, the portrait which emerged of America was oversimplified. Hollywood films customarily repress the nuances of society and history, as we have seen, but Gump seemed to provide a convenient excuse to repress more sophisticated, and more liberal, perspectives in favour of a narrow homespun conservatism. But the simplicity of such an ideology makes it seem a gut reaction to complex issues that deserve a more circumspect response. The fact is that many Americans can relate to homespun wisdom. Fewer wish to think through complex issues. After all, Hollywood films must end happily, all loose ends accounted for.

*Scene from* Forrest Gump

One legacy of the political turmoil of the 1960s and 1970s was the culture of political correctness. Keen to promote ideals of social diversity and inclusion in American society, advocates of PC attitudes among the political community, social reformers and the media sought to encourage such ideals by repressing certain usages of language and promoting others. Political correctness has touched upon media representations in the drive for social equality. *Independence Day* (Roland Emmerich, 1996) was the big summer release of its year. A blockbuster keen to maximize box-office receipts, it was bent upon appealing to a mass plural audience. Notice, therefore, that it is a Jew and an African American rather than a white Caucasian who save the world from aliens. Also appearing in 1996, the alien invasion movie *Mars Attacks!* (Tim Burton) not only paid homage to myriad alien invasion movies of the 1950s, but also ridiculed *Independence Day*'s attempt at political correctness. Here a trailer trash kid and a crazy old lady take the honours for saving the world! *One Fine Day* was also scrupulous in its inclusionary tactics. Elaine Lieberman's Hispanic maid cannot speak English so cannot assist Jack's search for Mrs Lieberman. But in case we might detect a patronizing attitude towards Hispanic Americans, Jack finds a Hispanic zoo warden who is more than capable of translating Spanish into English. Arguably, *Dangerous Minds* is a tribute to the contemporary culture of equal opportunity.

## Accusations against Hollywood

In 1992 Michael Medved's book *Hollywood vs. America* charged that Hollywood films undermine 'traditional family values'. That phrase again. Widely reviewed and read, Medved's book fed into long-running American and British debates about how far Hollywood influences attitudes and behaviour. Purporting to represent the values of America's Moral Majority, a middle-class constituency whose Christian and conservative outlook Medved saw as America's ideological backbone, his book even possessed a title which tapped into a widely shared belief that Hollywood has been out to corrupt America.

Real experience is the terrain over which Hollywood movies compete with the representations of experience in newspapers, history books, literature and cinemagoers' perspectives. As we know, film is a powerful medium of communication, and Hollywood's influential vision of the United States has always been of concern to politicians, businessmen and moralists. Angry petitions, industrial embargoes and direct censorship of Hollywood product have a long history in the United States and Britain.

American film history has generated a range of interesting and sometimes amusing anecdotes around the interface between Hollywood representation and public life. When big star Clark Gable removed his shirt in the romantic comedy *It Happened One Night* (Frank Capra, 1934) and he wasn't wearing a vest, sales of vests plummeted among American men! Fears of the pernicious influence of Hollywood films were boosted in the 1920s by a series of scandals involving stars' personal lives. This is significant insofar as it reflected the link in public perceptions between the lifestyles of Hollywood insiders and the content of Hollywood films. If to the moral majority in small towns across America Hollywood films were rife with sex and violence, Hollywood itself was a fleshpot. Introduced by the film industry to head off potential censorship from outside, the Production Code, or Hays Code (after its first chief administrator Will H. Hays), set out guidelines intended principally to curb the explicit representation of sex and violence on screen. By today's standards, these rules seem absurd. Married couples had to occupy separate beds, for instance. Violent death had to be practically bloodless. Criminal behaviour could not be represented in detail lest it provided inspiration for copycat offences. Put in place in 1934, the Production Code shaped Hollywood depictions of experience until the 1960s. The curbing of studio output is noticeable. We tend to think you don't 'see anything' in old black-and-whites, but there was a time just before the code came into force when Hollywood films were startlingly explicit. *Red-headed Woman* (Jack Conway, 1932) is a good example of a sexy pre–Production Code movie. In it an ambitious young woman, played by the alluring and sexually frank Jean Harlow, commits adultery with the boss in order to secure her future.

During the 1930s and 1940s, the interaction between the Code Administration's 'advice' to producers and filmic depiction was skilfully managed so as to serve simultaneously the lure of the poster and the obligations of public morality. Catering to a mass audience, producers found ways of getting around restrictions by appealing to both 'innocent' and 'sophisticated' readings. In the adventure romance *Casablanca* (Michael Curtiz, 1943), for example, the possibility that the hero and heroine sleep together can either be confirmed or denied, depending upon who was watching, as individual scenes are ambiguous on this point. The Production Code guideline stipulated that crime does not pay. So when *Double Indemnity* set out a 'blueprint for murder', in the Hays Office's words, the killers had to be killed off in the final reel. During World War II, the 'woman's picture' genre catered to audiences of American and British women eager for escape from workaday lives in the aircraft plants and munitions

▶ The moral guardians like to assume that the audience, whether at the cinema or at home, is helpless before the excessive imagery of the film. But why are we any more 'helpless' before a film than before a Shakespeare play or Stravinsky's *Rite of Spring*, a piece of music now performed regularly in concert halls, but described as obscene when it was first performed? ●

The woman's picture can also be read against the grain. See these melodramas in one light and they support the ideology of 'family values'. See them in another and they subvert it.

▶ Why were they called women's pictures? ●

A rich literature on the genre grew up in the 1970s and 1980s around writers such as Laura Mulvey, Mary Ann Doane and Jackie Stacey.

factories. The woman's picture offered the heroine (and the women who identified with her in the audience) escape from dull husbands, and love and sex with a handsome stranger – as long as the Production Code's injunction against adultery was observed in the final reel.

In the 1950s, films increasingly challenged Code restrictions. In 1953 the romantic comedy *The Moon Is Blue* (Otto Preminger) dared to use the banned term 'virgin' to describe the heroine. From the mid 1950s films such as the biker drama *The Wild One* (Laszlo Benedek, 1953) and the melodrama *Rebel without a Cause* (Nicholas Ray, 1955) revolved around that difficult and strange new breed, the 'teenager'. Female sexuality and teenage rebellion have always been hot topics for Hollywood films because sexuality and social rebellion challenge ideological norms and are considered 'dangerous', and are hence attractive to audiences. The allure of *Dangerous Minds* depends on such an appeal. These films offer the opportunity for audiences to live vicariously, then have their minds made up through a reassertion of family values, thus serving the dominant ideology. Until the rise of feminist thinking in the 1970s, official American and British assumptions about women revolved around ideals of nurturing mothers and dutiful wives, as opposed to the liberated and sexual individual we now realize each woman can be. That postwar clashes between the studios and Production Code administrators, and more recently between Hollywood distributors and moralists, have revolved around depictions of highly sexual women and so-called 'difficult' teenagers reflects public concern about social groups which since the 1960s have gained an increasing sense of identity.

As the women's movement challenged perceptions of women's roles in the 1960s, television brought the real violence of the Vietnam War and the American civil rights struggle into both American and British living rooms. The emergence of television as a mass medium in the 1950s and 1960s coincided with a decline in the old family movie audience, changes in the moral climate, and the beginnings of youth-oriented Hollywood genres and aesthetics. Code strictures relaxed, and the Production Code was eventually abolished in 1968.

In Britain a system of censorship has turned upon what was perceived as the undesirable influence of Hollywood

▶ Who created the upheaval in *Pleasantville* (Gary Ross, 1998)? Women and teenagers … Do you think this was intentional? Why? ●

▶ Can you think of a woman director whose representations of women's experiences effectively counter male-dominated film-making? Why? ●

films on youth. In 1917, the British Board of Film Censors (BBFC, 'Classification' from 1985), an industry-run advisory body founded in 1912, stipulated its opposition to 'the third degree American police interrogation method' and 'excessive revolver shooting'. During World War I (1914–18), police blamed growing juvenile delinquency on films, a development coinciding with film exhibitors' attempts to attract respectable middle-class audiences. In the 1940s and 1950s juvenile delinquency was cited in BBFC opposition to such films as the gangland drama *Brighton Rock* (John Boulting, 1947) and the abduction thriller *No Orchids for Miss Blandish* (St John L. Clowes, 1948). Censors removed the knife fight in *Rebel without a Cause* in 1956. *The Wild One* was not released in British cinemas until 1967.

The injunction against revolver shooting is a revealing one. Britain is Hollywood's chief export market, and therefore the influence of American films has been felt by audiences, and by moralists, for decades. Trading in graphic violence and an amorality associated at the time with cheap American 'pulp' literature, the Boulting and Clowes films spoke to moralists of a decline in standards which they associated with the increased influence of American culture on Britain in the immediate postwar period. Indeed, in an infamous case in 1955, Ruth Ellis's shooting of her lover was interpreted in terms of the pernicious influence of the United States on a society in which police did not carry firearms and, on the whole, neither did criminals. But, as in the United States, the cinema in Britain has traditionally been regarded as entertainment rather than art, a perception reflected in BBFC efforts to suppress politically awkward (usually foreign) films during and between the wars. Yet close examination of Board decisions in the area of political film at this time also reveals an insular attachment to the idea of an imperial 'Great' Britain in glorious isolation from all outside influences. The opposition to Hollywood 'trash', as opposed to British 'quality' film-making, persists in the popular imagination and continues to influence BBFC decisions and the pronouncements of moralists and critics.

The 1980s saw the end of a period of liberalization in British public and cultural life that began in the 1960s. The election of Margaret Thatcher in 1979 signalled widespread moral retrenchment which was reflected in BBFC decisions.

► Ask yourself why genre movies might be considered more dangerous than 'quality' films. ●

The police 'search and destroy' mission to seize a series of videos, including *I Spit on Your Grave* (Meir Zarchi, 1978) and *The Last House on the Left* (Wes Craven, 1972), under the Obscene Publications Act, was symptomatic of the new climate. Notice that these films are genre horror movies, as opposed to prestige films with strong literary or establishment credentials such as *The Madness of King George* (Nicholas Hytner, 1994) or *Four Weddings and a Funeral* (Mike Newell, 1993), and you get some sense of the mainstream predilections of British censors. In 1987 the Hungerford incident in which Michael Ryan went on a shooting rampage was blamed on the first *Rambo* films (George Pan Cosmatos, 1984/1985). More than a minute was removed from the theatrical version of *Rambo III* (Peter MacDonald, 1988).

The spread of the domestic VCR in the early 1980s saw renewed concern over Hollywood's influence. The Jamie Bulger murder case in 1994 fuelled a tabloid newspaper campaign against so-called 'video nasties'. Certification of the 'hood crime drama *Menace II Society* (Albert & Allen Hughes, 1993) was delayed until 1994. The same year Paul Dacre, editor of the *Daily Mail*, demanded that *Natural Born Killers* (Oliver Stone, 1994) 'be banned from Britain', although he had not actually seen it himself. It was subsequently passed uncut.

▶ What are we to make of the *Daily Mail* editor's objections to *Natural Born Killers*? ●

In 1914 'outrages against women' was added to the BBFC's list of exceptions. Since the slasher movie prototype *Psycho* (Alfred Hitchcock, 1960) brought sexual violence of a newly explicit kind to mainstream audiences, sexual violence against women has become an increasingly sensitive issue. In the 1970s the emergence of the slasher genre in *Halloween* (John Carpenter, 1978), *Dressed to Kill* (Brian DePalma, 1980) and others led feminists to take a stand. In the United States groups of women picketed cinemas playing *Dressed to Kill*. Sexual violence remains the main reason why adult censorship is still levied against film and video in Britain.

▶ Why do you think the issue of sexual violence against women should be such a sensitive one? ●

Such disputes and public outcries usually revolve around specific scenes deemed a pernicious influence because they are 'excessive'. But there are scenes in Shakespeare and in Greek tragedy that are appallingly violent. Yet these works are part of a recognized canon and are regularly performed. Until Film Studies became an accepted and proper subject of study in universities in the 1970s and 1980s, the cinema was widely regarded among social reformers, educators and guardians of taste as a lower form of art, trash for a mass audience. In Britain films and television are still widely seen as products rather than expressions of the aesthetic and moral temper of a particular society at a particular historical moment (as the unthinking recycling of distributor hype in critical reviews tends to illustrate!).

A recurring characteristic of the self-appointed moral guardian's dispute over screen violence and excessive sexual content in films is a personal preference for other sorts of texts. Violent and explicit films do not conform to a certain view of what films should be, according to our moral guardians. Time and time again, objections are mounted without first-hand knowledge of the film being debated. But as a student of Film Studies you already realize that all moving picture texts are worthy of close scrutiny for their aesthetics and for what they tell us about ourselves. Indeed, what has become known as the 'media effects debate' has now found its way onto the screen via the scene, for example, in which Film Studies students discuss the effects of screen violence in *Scream 2*.

The distinction between high art and low trash which is at the heart of many censorship disputes reveals much about the ideologies which prevail in British and American societies at a given moment. Coinciding with the rise of Film Studies was the growing perception of the film director as artist. In the 1990s public concern over the 'New Violence' of such films as *Reservoir Dogs* (Quentin Tarantino, 1992) and *Natural Born Killers* coalesced around the right of personal expression which society should accord directors such as Tarantino and Oliver Stone. It is a debate which still goes on whenever an ultra-violent film such as *Kill Bill* (Tarantino, 2003) appears.

*Scene from* Kill Bill

## Accusations against the director

Steven Spielberg is a director with mainstream respectability, almost an institution in Britain and the United States. When *Saving Private Ryan* (1998) gave rise to debate in the British and American press about the realism of its male dynamics, Spielberg was keen not only to depict war in all its messy and tragic violence, but also for wartime veterans to endorse his vision. To that end, screenings were organized for veterans' associations, and veterans were invited to attend tryouts.

However, it is the plea of self-expression rather than social responsibility that is the one most often invoked by directors. Self-expression has a long and tortuous history in Hollywood. After it was linked to violent crime in Britain, the political satire *A Clockwork Orange* (Stanley Kubrick, 1971) was withdrawn from British cinemas by Stanley Kubrick himself. Responding to the critical success of European art films in the United States and Britain, and amid a growing perception among British and American critics and audiences that Hollywood directors could be artists in their own right, the film director became an important cultural figure in the 1960s and 1970s. The theory and culture of the director as *auteur* ('author') has gained wide currency in Britain and America since French theorists formulated the *politique des auteurs* (loosely translated as the 'auteur theory') in the 1950s. Since then, American directors such as Kubrick, Martin Scorsese, Steven Spielberg, Oliver Stone and independents Robert Altman, Jim Jarmusch and Kevin Smith have come to be seen as artists to rank with writers and composers. The ideology of 'auteurism' underpinned the burgeoning respectability of the cinema and Film Studies, and, despite a range of new theoretical challenges, now underpins much critical writing and discussion, as well as the marketing of new films. The growth of arthouse cinema circuits since the 1960s is predicated institutionally and commercially upon this perspective on film production and reception. By withdrawing his work, Kubrick reserved the right to control its exhibition and interpretation.

Hollywood studios are in the business of making films that make money. Hence they are concerned with appealing widely, and placating public fears over content and its reception. Through repeated commercial and critical success, some directors have managed to overcome the tension between making money for the studio and its stockholders and making a personal statement in their films. The history of Hollywood could be read as a long-running tussle between the corporate executives' need to balance the books and the maverick director's desire to express himself. Disputes have turned upon claims about the efficiency of representation and the authenticity of the personal vision. While studios have complained about non-commercial unhappy endings,

---

After *The Godfather* (1971) made a pot of money for Paramount, the studio rewarded director Francis Ford Coppola with the go-ahead to make an arthouse film for himself. But some directors, having pleased the studio executives and confronted with the luxury of expressing themselves, have been so seduced by commercial success and the swimming pool that comes with it that they could not be bothered to make an arthouse film.

▶ What would you do in their position? ●

unorthodox characterizations, aesthetically risky shooting and editing strategies, directors have sought to challenge Hollywood representations and send a message about the human condition.

Director Orson Welles famously got into trouble with studio RKO in 1941 over his depiction of the newspaper tycoon William Randolph Hearst in *Citizen Kane*. After unsuccessfully attempting to buy and destroy Welles's film, Hearst ensured that none of his newspapers carried an advertisement for *Citizen Kane*. Imagine if Oliver Stone made a film featuring a thinly disguised depiction of contemporary media mogul Rupert Murdoch, and you get some idea of the impact of *Citizen Kane* when it appeared. As controller of BSkyB and a range of newspapers, Murdoch is responsible for the far-reaching spread of ideological messages and assumptions. In the 1940s, 1950s and 1960s, Billy Wilder's films frequently upset studio executives and censors for their risky treatments of sexual relationships. Stories of budget overruns and logistical excess abounded while Francis Ford Coppola filmed *Apocalypse Now* (1979), a film which wrought financial and psychological havoc, not least on the director himself.

The past twenty years have seen the rise of the 'director's cut', a re-released version of an earlier successful film, recut and modified according to the director's wishes. Now an institution, the director's cut acknowledges the perennial tug between corporate fiat and directorial vision which lies at the heart of American cinema. In 2000 *Apocalypse Now Redux* appeared, a recut version of the original which not only represented the opportunity for Coppola to exhibit the vision he had originally intended, but resurrected a classic film for fresh returns at the box office as well. When his science-fiction thriller *Blade Runner* (1982) was first screened for the executives, Ridley Scott was required to re-edit the film, add a romantic ending and a voice-over narration to the soundtrack because studio executives believed cinemagoers would not be able to follow it. Appearing in 1991, *Blade Runner: The Director's Cut* found the cuts reinstated and the voice-over removed.

As we know, the 1990s saw the rise of the US independent sector and the appearance of a range of films and auteurs whose visions respond to the mainstream ideological

▶ Pick a film you really like. Make a case for its ideological content based upon reading it on an implicit level. ●

solutions of Hollywood with quirky and seemingly amoral perspectives on experience. Ideologically, the American cinema has come a long way from the moral straitjacket of the Production Code, with directors from Robert Altman to Terry Zwigoff conjuring singular universes to rank with the unconventional perspectives of the European cinema.

# 5. Realist Movements and Traditions

*In chapters 1 to 4 we looked at the particular realism which we associate with Hollywood film-making and the multiplex experience. Hollywood has provided one model for mainstream realist aesthetics wherever they are found. In chapters 5 and 6 we shall look at realist movements and traditions from other parts of the world. As with US independent cinema, these models are characteristic of arthouse exhibition fare in Britain, so the expectations which these films set up in the audience tend to be different from the purely narrative and entertainment-based expectations of Hollywood films. The central role which Hollywood realism has assumed throughout film history is witnessed by the fact that arthouse films, be they European, Iranian or British, owe their specific characters to the ways in which they differ from Hollywood in their treatment of real experience.*

## French poetic realism

As we shall see, the emergence of cinematic realisms tends to coincide with a change in the political climate in favour of populist policies and ideology. Like many realist movements, French poetic realism was linked to certain historical moments as socialist governments and outlooks replaced conservative regimes. French poetic realism developed in the 1930s as the expression of a specifically French aesthetic and moral sensibility linked to nineteenth-century literature which was encouraged by a changing political climate, and the collapse of commercial studio conglomerates which had dominated the French film industry.

This book does not seek to encourage a distinction between Hollywood and 'art' or foreign-language films, any more than it distinguishes between so-called 'quality' cinema and genre movies, or canonical films and cult movies.

The more you practise Film Studies, the more you will come across films with a Film Studies agenda. You may like these films on a personal level. Or you may prefer others. All films are, in their own way, realist, and all are equally worthy of study.

▶ As a member of the audience, how far does the atmosphere of the arthouse cinema shape your reception of what you see there? ●

The rise of poetic realism is related to the rise and fall of the Popular Front, a consolidation of left-wing parties and factions which came to power in 1936. For many, the Popular Front represented the possibility of far-reaching social reforms. But owing to an adverse economic climate and the looming possibility of war with Germany, the Popular Front achieved little. While key poetic realist films revolve around working men and women, they are pessimistic in mood and often end tragically.

Unusually for realist cinema, poetic realism was studio-based, its portraits of ordinary experience generated from the conventions of screenwriting and camerawork, sets, lighting and actors available to small independent producers. Real locations and non-professional actors figure little in the evolution of the style. Streets and rooms in Paris were meticulously rebuilt in the studio. As the name suggests, poetic realism attempted to combine the realistic with the lyrical or emotional, showing how the poetic could arise out of the situations and dimensions of everyday life. In a cheap room, a murderer waits to die in *Le Jour se lève* (*Daybreak*, Marcel Carné, 1939), his redemption his love for a woman. *Le Crime de M Lange* (*M Lange's Crime*, Jean Renoir, 1935) tells of a publishing company which flourishes as a workers cooperative following the shooting of the grasping publisher. In *Hotel du Nord* (Marcel Carné, 1938), two lovers pledge to commit suicide together.

The generation of poetic or lyrical elements out of the grubby facts of life anticipated realist movements from Italian neo-realism to the British New Wave of the 1950s and 1960s. Indeed, key poetic realist director Jean Renoir was invited to teach at Rome's Centro Sperimentale del Cinema film school in 1939, a seedbed for neo-realism. Many realist tendencies were also characterized by their attention to the suffering of male protagonists, a preoccupation that answered socio-historical and institutional shifts. Often telling of desperate men experiencing emotional turmoil or on the run, the poetic realists' use of side-lighting and part-lighting fragments faces in order to suggest inner conflict. Claustrophobic sets and the symbolic use of particular objects add to the tension.

The French poetic realists' impact on our expectations and understanding of realism generally has occurred at the level of content and outlook. An enduring perception of cinematic realism wherever it has occurred has been that it portrays urban life. The night streets, dingy apartments, working-class *arrondissements* and docklands in these films continue to shape what we think of as realist film-making, whether Italian neo-realism, American film noir or the films of the British New Wave.

## Italian neo-realism

The most famous realist movement in film history, Italian neo-realism was the first major European alternative to the Hollywood realist aesthetic to appear after World War II. Not simply a new way of making films, neo-realism had a moral and political dimension. Emerging out of Italy's experience of fascist dictatorship, war, military occupation and economic hardship, neo-realist directors sought to turn all this into a new kind of unadulterated aesthetic, one that showed the world as it really is. As a movement, neo-realism lasted only a few short years. But as an aesthetic, its influence on films and television has been felt from *EastEnders* to *Kandahar* (Mohsen Makhmalbaf, 2001). Like other realist movements throughout film history, neo-realism arose organically out of other styles, but real Italian history lies at the heart of its distinctive flavour.

*Ossessione* (*Obsession*, Luchino Visconti, 1942) is generally regarded as the first neo-realist film, a tale of adultery and murder filmed against the dusty backdrop of the Delta Ferrarese in northern Italy. Director Luchino Visconti had been an assistant to Jean Renoir, whose 1934 film *Toni* took place amid the Italian immigrant community of southern France. Shot on location employing non-professional actors and using diegetic sound only, rather than adding a soundtrack later in the studio, this melodramatic story of sexual passion and murder was similar to that found in *Ossessione*, with Renoir's methods drawing out the simple humanity and poetry of everyday life. The combination of pathos and verisimilitude is common in neo-realist films such as *Rome, Open City* (Roberto Rossellini, 1945).

Financed from beyond the official Italian film industry and employing non-professional actors using a collectively written script, *Rome, Open City* told the true story of a priest executed by the Nazis for his resistance activities. Shot on the

*In Chapter 1 you were asked if you have ever watched a scene in a film in which ordinary people do ordinary things, and wondered why you were riveted by it. Watching a neo-realist film can be a similarly transfixing, even passionately involving, experience. Theorist and screenwriter Cesare Zavattini (1902–89) once wrote of wanting to make a film about a man to whom nothing ever happens!*

*So outraged was the fascist government by Ossessione's authentic account of the desires of ordinary men and women that an archbishop was called in to sprinkle holy water on the cinema where it opened. Suppressed from international distribution by Hollywood major MGM (which based its The Postman Always Rings Twice (1946) on the same source), an uncut version of the film was not shown in the United States until 1976.*

*'The reality buried under the myths slowly reflowered. The cinema began its creation of the world. Here was a tree; here an old man; here a house; here a man eating, a man sleeping, a man crying.' (Cesare Zavattini)*

streets of Rome in the places where these events actually took place during the final months of World War II, even as the Germans occupied precincts of the city, the film owes its uneven look to the stock having to be bought from street photographers. To keep the production cheap, sound was added after the footage had been shot. Recruited on the spot, some of the amateur actors died while production was taking place. The impression we get is of a story picked up and left to continue after the film has ended.

The scene in which the Germans search for resistance figures house to house is full of incidental detail just as real life is. A little choirboy kicks a German soldier. Another soldier molests Pina as she is made to stand with the evacuated women. Meanwhile, the camera observes. First the streets filling with soldiers as you or I might witness it from a window. Then the actual apartments, staircases and courtyards as the soldiers clatter past. It is as though this is just another dull day in a forgotten district made briefly exciting by these events. Although the actual scene of Pina's death is dramatized by cutting from her to her husband being driven away, then to Don Pietro comforting Pina's son, the shots that kill her seem to come from nowhere. We hear a crack – it could be a car backfiring in the next street – we see her fall – we make the connection. You must have noticed how in real life you register sounds before associating them with seen events. We notice most of all a long ladder in Pina's stockings when she is lying there in the road, a commonplace enough detail amid tragic circumstances. No dramatic cry, no blood, the whole episode over in seconds just as we have seen in actuality footage of, say, the Kennedy assassination.

What is transfixing about the scene in which Pina dies is that the everyday event comes to seem historical. We are witnessing the ordinary, yet its immediacy makes the everyday into a particular day. Experience may not have today's date written all over it, but, if a film, or a photograph, captures the circumstances, the sensations, the sounds, the light, it models reality in such a way as to enable us to experience 'experience' more vividly. Notice how Pina shrieks when Francesco is carried away. Notice how her hair blows as she rushes towards the truck. Actor Anna Magnani's whole body becomes seized with Pina's need to catch up with the speeding truck so that only a bullet will stop her.

Rome, Open City: *Pina is dying …*

Pina has seldom lived as intensely as she is living her last few moments. But as in a photograph of action stopped dead, she is now stopped dead. Everyday life in all its vivid detail. It becomes a moment worthy of historical record. Someday we are all going to be experiencing life in all its vivid detail. Then we will become history, part of a day that will never be repeated.

The neo-realists were active during a period when Italy was transformed from a fascist dictatorship to a democracy, albeit defeated and steeped in poverty. Since 1922, Italy had been a totalitarian state under Benito Mussolini. Recognizing the power of film as a tool of propaganda, Mussolini had the huge Cinecittà studios (pronounced chin-eh-chitt-*ah*) built on the outskirts of Rome in emulation of Hollywood, and established the Italian Film School. Committed to film-making which would promote his new Italy to the outside world and to the Italian people, the regime sponsored polished middle-class melodramas which came to be known contemptuously as 'white telephone movies' because of the plush white telephones found in every penthouse and hotel suite. To preserve the spotlessness of Mussolini's new Italy, Italian films would feature no crime and no 'immorality'. There were, however, directors and screenwriters in the industry who began to rebel against such derivative and constraining aesthetics.

In 1943 as Italy was liberated from fascist control by American and British forces, conditions briefly obtained whereby a new kind of film-making could blossom. Directors turned their cameras on the grubby realities of Italian urban life: the itinerant poor, the bombed-out apartments, children begging, soup kitchens, soldiers, prostitutes. In place of the glossy studio-produced 'worlds' of fascist cinema, the neo-realists introduced practices that would bring the real Italy to the screen. Although they did not publish a manifesto as other movements such as the Dogme 95 directors did in the 1990s, the original neo-realist films embodied neo-realist practices.

French theorist André Bazin (1918–58) championed neo-realism for embodying the revelatory, or photographic, capacity of a camera trained on life itself. The neo-realists seemed to reveal an already existing reality, rather than creating 'reality' in the camera *for* the camera, as Hollywood films did. Italian films literally recorded a slice of life, the

*You might argue that the Italian fascists' notion of 'immorality' bears resemblance to contemporary Anglo-American notions of 'family values'.*

*'The Italian camera retains something of the human quality of the Bell and Howell newsreel camera, a projection of hand and eye, almost a living part of the operator, instantly in tune with his awareness.' (André Bazin, 1948)*

camera entering actual experience. There would be no literary adaptations. The focus would be on the face of Italian society as the neo-realists found it. Dialogue and language should be natural, employing regional dialects and non-professional actors, even if sometimes dubbed by professionals. Real locations would be used rather than studio facilities. The shooting style would be documentary, using natural light, hand-held cameras, observation and analysis of the scene as the film found it. Key neo-realist Roberto Rossellini shot crowds at random at the scene of the action. The heroine of the first story of the liberation drama *Paisà* (pronounced: paee-*za*) (Roberto Rossellini, 1946) was an illiterate found on the dockside. Anna Magnani was an actor formerly associated with 'café-concert', a tradition of theatre and public performance committed to the popular and vernacular expression of experience. The girl in *Rome, Open City*, Maria Michi, was found working in a cinema. Bazin may have exaggerated the neo-realists' use of long takes (in which the camera is left to run without cutting), and fluid camera movements that preserved the sense of a real continuous space, but his reverence for their moral project of returning to an honest and humane aesthetic is justified. Although *Bicycle Thieves* (Vittorio De Sica, 1948) revolves around nothing more complex than a man losing his bike – his livelihood and his stature in the eyes of his son depend upon it – owing to the way the film unfolds organically as everyday life does, it remains compelling to watch. The neo-realist legacy can be felt into 1960s Italian cinema in the work of Visconti – *Rocco and His Brothers* (1960) – and Francesco Rosi – *Salvatore Giuliano* (1961).

The best neo-realism displays a regard for and a responsibility towards real experience such that watching it you feel as though you have seen a film that was actually *about* something. With their dramatic music and histrionic acting, works such as *Ossessione*, *Rome, Open City* and *Bicycle Thieves* may seem melodramatic to us today; however, the shift from the middle-class preoccupations of prewar Italian cinema to the locations and protagonists of a ravaged postwar Italy imparted a genuine sense of immediacy to postwar critics and audiences. These films constituted an influential attempt to find solutions to issues of representation that would be tackled differently in different countries in

*Also influenced by the neo-realists was Indian director Satyajit Ray. Evincing a meditative style and a deep understanding of Bengali village life, Ray deployed an intent, unobtrusive camera, discreet and economical editing and close observation of the faces of the poverty-stricken. Pather Panchali (1955) is a portrait of village life seen through the eyes of a six-year-old. It won an award as the 'best human documentary' at the Cannes Film Festival.*

▶ Is it so important that films be 'about' something in this sense? Or is entertainment more important than relevance? ●

▶ Great aesthetic leaps often take place at times of turmoil. Do you think that these aesthetic leaps are worth it, given the hardship out of which they emerged? Or do you think we should forget about the hardship and concentrate on the movies? Why? ●

subsequent ... -realism's unscripted style and ... ack-and-white and alive with the ... urban communities still seem to ... when we talk about realism.

... explored the potential of real ... were taking place in the United ... that gave rise to a style of film- ... ditional Hollywood realism. A ... etic currents contributed to a ... ch appeared roughly between ... known as 'film noir' (black ... to the emergence of film noir ... and content of these films. ... battles, in 1948 the US Supreme ... trust suit against the Hollywood studios. ... Paramount Consent Decree' instructed the companies to divest themselves of their cinema holdings, effectively breaking the vertically integrated monopoly of production, distribution and exhibition that they had held since the 1920s. This meant that the studios had to go into competition with newly emerging independent producers to provide cinemas with films.

Rising costs during this period combined with falling income drove the studios to economise. With a reputation for healthy audience response and potentially lucrative scenarios heavy on sex and violence, film noir pushed the boundaries of what mainstream films could show. The sale and recycling of expensive sets by the rising TV networks, exploitation of documentary film stock archives, and the shorter shooting times afforded by such contemporary dramas made them attractive to the major studios and smaller independents alike. Throughout film history, realist shifts have been motivated by new technology. Increasingly sensitive fine-grain negatives, high-speed lenses, smaller camera dollies and portable power supplies perfected for wartime newsreel footage made shooting away from the studio an exciting alternative, creating films with a topical edge. New negatives and lenses meant less light was needed to expose the film, making night shooting a viable alternative, and lending these films their characteristically dark and gloomy look.

'Its figures are The Accused, Abandoned, Cornered, Framed, Railroaded, Convicted, Caged and Desperate.' (Alain Silver in Film Noir: An Encyclopedic Reference Guide, p. 4)

Double Indemnity: *cinema of nightfall*

Although the United States had come out of World War II on the winning side, the immediate postwar years are characterized by a mood of fear and paranoia. Indirectly examined in film noir are the unspoken fears – war guilt, the rise of a female workforce, white suburbs versus black ghettoes – emerging from between the lines of America's postwar triumphalism. Sex, violence and working-class milieux characterize postwar film noir, while, as so often in film history, altering industrial conditions made for a liberalization of technique and style. Film noir scenarios provided exciting and poignant vehicles for exorcising the bad dreams of returning servicemen, soothing sexual and economic insufficiency, and allaying the concerns of ordinary Americans in a politically altering world. The possibility that political enmity between the United States and the Soviet Union might result in the destruction of life as we know it hung over the postwar world like a recurring nightmare. During the war years American women gained a significant measure of economic independence by working in aircraft factories, stores and public transport. Anxiety over the erosion of men's traditional place as breadwinners fed into film noir's climate of suspicion and physical and emotional violence. Mediating post-conflict trauma found lonely men up against forces they fail to understand, these films reaching deep into the social undergrowth in search of the painful burden of victory. *Double Indemnity* (Billy Wilder, 1944) contains graphic levels of violence which, like the gritty locations common to film noir, are symptomatic of a newly expanding mainstream vision.

*Double Indemnity* exemplifies the currents that played into film noir. The film charts in flashback the story of an adulterous couple who kill her husband for a lucrative insurance settlement. Set against the backdrop of the Spanish-style villas, suburban shopping malls and railroad yards that dot outer Los Angeles, and pervaded with a sense of romantic doom, *Double Indemnity* owes its grubby locations and fatalistic temper to both the French poetic realists of the 1930s and the bleak urban settings of neo-realism. The vernacular dialogue and the presence of Edward G. Robinson, an actor associated with the Hollywood gangster movie cycle of the 1930s, also saw film noir fed by earlier American realist sensibilities. The production's use of real Los Angeles streets and supermarket locations signalled a burgeoning trend in postwar Hollywood film-making.

Its adulterous relationship and detailed murder plot meant that *Double Indemnity* was dubbed by the then Head of the Production Code, Joseph Breen, as a 'blueprint for murder'. But scraping by with minor modifications, the film came to be regarded by audiences and executives as a watershed in the representation of seedy lifestyles. Although film noir did not feature significantly among box-office successes during the 1940s and 1950s, films in this genre did take advantage of more sophisticated audience targeting and communicated to a younger audience eager to see films with challenging content that seemed to explain the modern generation's thoughts and feelings. Countering the quiet domesticity and staid lifestyles of middle-class suburbanites, film noir had an aura of moral ambivalence associated with urban life that was considered very romantic.

If 'high' film noir explored the fraught psychologies of men on the edge of an affluent postwar society, the 'neo-noirs' of the 1960s and since portrayed men even more detached from the America they see around them. *Point Blank* (John Boorman, 1967) follows the dreamlike odyssey of an ex-convict bent on finding and killing the man who stole his money. Shot against the backdrop of the extreme modernist architecture of contemporary Los Angeles, Walker's revenge takes him further and further into an illusory world of Polaroid towers and corporate bonhomie. Neo-noir's realism consists of both its bold attempt to inhabit the concrete parking lots, freeways and high-rise apartments of modern America, and one man's desperate perspective on all this. On the face of it a highly stylized film for its use of locations, actors and colour, *Point Blank* is significant for pointing towards postwar European and American attempts to map character psychology on to objective experience. This is a project that the American independents of the 1990s took very seriously.

## The French New Wave and contemporary realisms

The year 1959 was something of a watershed in world cinema and saw the emergence of new waves across Europe. None is more renowned than the French New Wave. Born in 1958, the Fifth Republic was bent upon modernizing French society

▶ How often are you watching a film when your eye is caught by what's going on in the background? What motivates your interest? ●

and its institutions, including the cinema, always seen as vital to the national heritage. As directors such as Carné and Renoir aged, younger men were encouraged into the industry. Around 170 film-makers made their debut features between 1959 and 1963. They included directors who would revolutionize French and world cinema.

New Wave film-makers were reacting against what they saw as an outmoded cinema encrusted with the scenarios, conventions and stars of the 1930s and 1940s. The new generation was the first to have been brought up in the age of cinema, and early works display genuine excitement about the possibilities of film. They took their cameras on to the streets and into the cafés, apartments and lives of young Parisians. They employed non-actors and those just starting out. They captured French youth at a particular moment. They chopped stories up or made them plotless like experience. They used jump cuts and ellipses that broke with industry convention and drew attention to the fact that fictional film is also a record of the reality of the film's making. They imported the trickery of silent cinema into the mix to give a heightened sense of the cinematic image's interface between record and aesthetic. They used 'low' sources such as French and American pulp novelettes and films, as opposed to the 'high' literary sources favoured during the classical period. They established a new pantheon of stars. No matter whether set in the present – *Breathless* (*À Bout de souffle*, Jean-Luc Godard, 1959) – or in the past – *Jules et Jim* (François Truffaut, 1961) – New Wave films always seemed to be set in the here and now.

Epitomizing the fresh and vibrant aspirations of this new cinema, *Breathless* followed the fortunes of a fugitive gangster and his girlfriend, its naturalistic acting, ragged editing and camerawork catching each emotional and cultural nuance of their world. *Jules et Jim* relates the ups and downs of two friends and the woman they both love over a long period. Constantly changing mood and tone, both of these films push the envelope of what can be shown and explored in films. When they appeared, they seemed as lively and shapeless as experience itself.

The most prominent New Wave directors, among them Godard, Truffaut and Claude Chabrol, had been critics writing for the magazine *Cahiers du cinéma*, a publication committed to the philosophy of the director as auteur. 'Auteurism' was a rationale elaborated in the pages of *Cahiers* which was intended to celebrate the classical Hollywood studio product that was then finding its way into French cinemas. Its premise was that the director was the key creative agency in the making of a film and any aesthetic value a film possessed was due to his efforts. New Wave films, therefore, tended to privilege personal style in their look and in the confessional and philosophical nature of their narratives and content. In this respect, they have hugely influenced and shaped postwar realisms outside France.

Locating artistic value in the contribution of the director has had widespread appeal for critics and, not surprisingly, directors themselves since the 1960s, and auteurism now underpins much journalism and academic writing on the cinema. Chiming with the decline of faith in transcendent ethical values in modern life, as well as the decline of studio film-making, auteurism has seemed to validate directors' cinemas for their apparently genuine portrayals of experience, unmediated by the trappings of either commerce or ideology.

The main challenge to auteurist thinking has been that film-making is a collaborative industry and a film the result of myriad efforts by personnel and crew, while recent theory has brought the audience in as a maker of meaning. But as a discourse, auteurism has been so pervasive in industry and critical circles that the director's name has become a label for a product and a vision of experience. That the vision is one man's (women directors are still relatively few) seems symptomatic of the postwar problematizing of the 'objective', and widespread notions of postmodern ethical and cultural fragmentation. Although the New Wave introduced a new kind of economically and sexually liberated woman in Jeanne Moreau, Jean Seberg and Anna Karina, as if to mirror their auteurist philosophy, New Wave films tend to emphasize male outlooks and experience. Actors such as Jean-Paul Belmondo and Alain Delon epitomize this mood.

Part of the impetus for the rise of the French New Wave was the development of lightweight equipment and fast and cheap film stock in the 1950s. Like early television, which tended to be shot live, this technology introduces the sense of presence that we associate with realism. Postwar

▶ Is it right to prize freshness in what the camera sees? Why? After all, if you see it often enough it is going to become stale … ●

equipment built upon the transfixed witnessing of history that we associate with the scene of Pina's death in *Rome, Open City* by enabling the film-maker to admit more of the world into the shot. *Breathless* brings with it a sense of presence through its hand-held camerawork. Walking along the streets of Paris with Belmondo and Seberg, in 1959, Godard allows us to soak up the atmosphere of a particular moment in a particular spot along the Champs Élysées. You could watch this sequence over and over again and spot a specific event inadvertently filmed in the background. Nothing to do with Godard's narrative, it is nevertheless now part of the world of that narrative. Hence Godard places his film on the same level of incidental activity as the real life unfolding behind his actors. *Cinéma-vérité* (film truth) film-makers working at around the same time as the New Wave also fertilized the movement. As we shall see, *cinéma-vérité* directors made possible the capture of 'unofficial' and vernacular lives and histories.

Since the New Wave first broke, public funding has made incentives available to a widening range of directors in France. One film appeared in 1995 that drew attention to the rage of excluded French minorities and put this emotion in front of mainstream audiences both inside and outside France, drawing upon the distinctive *Arabe* or *beur* cinema, a 1980s current dealing with the lives of immigrant groups in France. The action of *La Haine* (*Hate*, Matthieu Kassovitz) takes place over twenty-four hours following the shooting of an Arab by Paris police. Three young men from the *banlieux* (poor suburbs), a Jew, an Arab and an Afro-Frenchman, come into possession of the gun used in the shooting. Shot in a jittery hand-held style and written in the *verlan* (slangy 'back talk') of an angry underclass, *La Haine* invested its thriller format with all the political urgency and significance of a rolling telecast.

Sandrine Veysset's *Will It Snow for Christmas?* (1996) is an autobiographically inspired account of the privations of life on a southern French farm which cuts through a certain kind of *cinéma de patrimoine* (nostalgic heritage cinema meant for export and typified by *Jean de Florette*, Claude Berri, 1986), in search of a non-judgmental account of poverty and abuse. Naturalistic in its performances, the camera puts you right in among the family.

*Will It Snow at Christmas?*: *The search for authenticity*

## Cinéma-vérité

*Cinéma-vérité* (cinema truth) is a translation of a Russian term *Kino Pravda*, given to the filmic equivalent of the Soviet Russian news journal *Pravda* by the 1920s film-maker Dziga Vertov. Inspired by the Russians, the *cinéma-vérité* movement consisted of a group of 1960s French film-makers who sought to put unmediated experience back on the screen. Recalling Bazin's observation of neo-realism, these directors tried to reveal, rather than capture, the 'truth' of a scene, according to the idea that real experience is all around us in all its ambiguity rather than contained in an essential state to be isolated from the real by the camera. Benefiting from the development of the transistor, portable light sources, the Swiss Nagra tape recorder, and the French Coutant camera in the 1950s, *cinéma-vérité* was concurrent with the fiction films of the French New Wave. It was also influenced by the burgeoning impact of TV news reportage.

However, as soon as the film-maker points the camera at anything they begin to bring attitudes and decisions to bear upon their material. Hence, there can really be no such thing as '*vérité*' in cinema. Ever since Dziga Vertov made *The Man with a Movie Camera* (1929), in which candid scenes of Moscow street life were filmed employing the trickery of the all-seeing camera, the camera's ability to see has been compromised by its ability to change what it sees.

Taking equipment on to the streets and recording the thoughts of private individuals introduces a plurality of hidden histories onto the screen, perhaps the most valuable legacy of any realist cinema. At around the time of *cinéma-vérité*, in the United States a related tendency, Direct Cinema, also evolved. Avoiding planned narrative of any kind, Direct Cinema film-makers got participants to expose their motives, attitudes and psychologies inadvertently. The camera and the director do not intervene. Zoom lenses were used to get close to people without interfering in the natural flow of speech or action. Directional microphones were used to catch talk from a distance.

Richard Leacock was a British-born cameraman who had worked with key documentarist Robert Flaherty on *Louisiana Story* (1948). Latterly working in television, Leacock tended to record events whose outcomes were open-ended. Having set up production facility Drew Associates

*On 22 November 1963, the assassination of President John F. Kennedy in Dallas, Texas, was caught on a 16mm home movie camera by onlooker Abraham Zapruder, gory details included. It has become not only a document of a violent century, but also a key moment in news reportage, one that foresaw the introduction of truly violent events into the living room every day on the evening news.*

▶ Compare and contrast *High School*'s treatment of the classroom with that in *Dangerous Minds*. ●

with Robert Drew, in the early 1960s Flaherty and Drew made films for ABC TV's Close Up! series, including *Primary* (1960), in which they followed then president-elect John F. Kennedy during his primary campaign against Hubert Humphrey in Wisconsin in 1960. Following Kennedy from town to town as he talks to voters, we naturally come to hope for his success. Introducing a tension unusual in documentary at that time, the significance of the actuality recorded only becomes apparent as shooting came to an end. Frederick Wiseman was a former law professor and lawyer whose knowledge of public institutions brought insight to *High School* (1968). Although a contemporary of the Direct Cinema film-makers, in his films Wiseman exhibits strong opinions about what his camera sees. Quietly observing the teacher–student relationship in the classrooms and along the corridors of an American high school, Wiseman shot hundreds of hours of footage to get an overall sense of reality before cutting it to accommodate his critique of the system.

With its frank and apparently unmediated observation of actual human behaviour, a drama built out of life's little incidents, *cinéma-vérité* remains arresting for its seemingly authoritative stance. We sit up and take notice when what we are watching is underwritten by the shaky camerawork, bland monochrome look and sober informational approach initiated by the *cinéma-vérité* film-makers. Emerging in the 1960s, a decade when left-wing radicals were active in social and political debates, *cinéma-vérité* has tended to become associated with political activism, adding to our sense that realism is a set of aims and aesthetics serving a socially progressive agenda.

## New Hollywood

In the late 1950s the French New Wave was a youth-oriented cinema which effectively rewrote the interface between film language and experience. As we saw in Chapter 4, the teenager became a recognized social and cultural group in the 1950s. Becoming increasingly independent and self-defining, this generation would be the audience for a new wave of American film-making. The traditional audience for the downtown 'picture theater' had by the early 1960s moved to the suburbs where it sat in front of the television.

Meanwhile, screenings of unconventional fare at drive-ins and by campus film societies fed the new generation's desire for something else.

In opposition to traditional Hollywood and in emulation of the new French auteur, 'New Hollywood' would be a director's cinema. The generation of American directors who emerged in the 1960s saw American cinema become diversified in style and appeal. Influenced by the stylish preoccupation with youth experience that they saw in European art cinema, these directors answered a new generation's demand for a cinema charting how it felt about American life, as well as its recognition that the lens frame defines as much as it reveals.

The year 1967 marked the appearance of the new sensibility with the release of *Bonnie and Clyde* (Arthur Penn). Like *Breathless* in 1959, it followed a criminal couple's exploits, dwelling with unusual candour upon their quirky sexual and emotional life. *Bonnie and Clyde* combined the energy of a cheap action movie and the vernacular of working-class middle America with the ironic distance associated with the European art film. At times reminiscent of slapstick comedy, at others steeped in ferocious violence, the film kept its audience constantly on edge. Resonating with the contemporary perception that violence was somehow integral to American life – seen every night in TV footage of the Vietnam War, every day at a mall or drugstore shooting – it answered the need for an American cinema that was rooted in American experience.

Another key moment in the emergence of the New Hollywood was the film *The Graduate* (Mike Nichols, 1967), which also responded to the experiences of young Americans. Nichols's film charted the uncertain sexual fortunes of a middle-class California university graduate as he decides what to do with his life. The film also tapped into modern youth's perplexed responses to American materialism, sexual mores and the mythos of 'family values'.

These films may have owed their zooms and telephoto lenses, their slow motion and split screens to the French New Wave, but their attempt to tackle the times, coupled with an emotionally dislocated, rebellious and populist attitude, brought a realism into American cinema which survives into the contemporary scene.

Kandahar: *Iranian neo-realism*

## Iranian cinema

One of the most striking developments of the 1990s was the emergence of a fresh, observant and intellectually stimulating cinema from Iran. Governed from 1979 by a stern and repressive Shi'ite Islamic regime, the country has seen a recent liberalization which has brought about a revolution in Iranian film-making.

The cinema is extremely popular in Iran. While many of the films which have appeared at international film festivals and in western metropolitan arthouse cinemas were not shown in Iranian cinemas, attendance for genre movies is high, and there is widespread fascination with the apparatus and cultures of cinema. When it reached Iran in the 1960s and 1970s, the work of the Italian neo-realists was highly regarded. Realism tempered with poetic sensibility and reflexive experiment are key characteristics of the new Iranian cinema.

The preoccupation with the fortunes of ordinary people as they deal with economic hardship, natural disaster, crime, and religious and gender oppression crop up across the Iranian oeuvre. Yet the manner in which these realities are observed often evinces an eye for the haunting and beautiful image, the offbeat event. For example, in *Kandahar* (Mohsen Makhmalbaf, 2001), set in Afghanistan against the backdrop of Taliban rule, an airdrop of artificial limbs floats through the sky as landmine casualties chase after them.

Consonant with the interest in cinema as an apparatus, the work of Abbas Kiarostami dissolves the tension between verisimilitude and formal film-making processes. Kiarostami

Director Mohsen Makhmalbaf's daughter Samira's first film *The Apple* (1998) was based upon a newspaper story about two sisters incarcerated by their father who finally emerge to make sense of the world around them. Its script following rather than preceding the film's shooting, this potent mix of documentary and fable could be seen as a metaphor for the emergence of a new Iran and its film-makers' attempt to interpret what they see around them.

often gives the script out to actors day by day, to keep them spontaneous. Kiarostami's children remind you of those wide-eyed kids in *Rome, Open City*, their innocent viewpoints emphasizing the injustices and oppression of Iranian society. Emerging from beneath the veil of patriarchal Islamic law, new Iranian cinema itself is an almost childlike celebration of cinema and its possibilities.

Film theorist Laura Mulvey (b. 1941) described Kiarostami's work as creating both curiosity and uncertainty in audiences about what is happening on screen. This can be quite striking for audiences used to the 'obvious' realism of Hollywood. In a trilogy of films set in the northern town of Koker, the director focuses upon the lives of ordinary Iranians in a community devastated by an earthquake in 1991. The sympathetic treatment of everyday peril can be found in *Where Is My Friend's House?* (1987), a neo-realist essay in which a young man embarks on a circuitous journey to return his friend's exercise book, ever in fear of the friend's expulsion from school. With its repetitive structure evoking real day-to-day experience, there is also a clever formalism at work here that anticipates Kiarostami's interest in the very project of making films. *And Life Goes On …* (1992) found the director back in Koker interviewing earthquake survivors and reflecting on the ethics of film-making. In *Through the Olive Trees* (1994), Kiarostami returns again to film a fictionalized account of the behind-the-scenes events taking place during the shooting of *And Life Goes On …*. Very little actually happens, but the vicissitudes of making movies (and finding love!) are explored in a long-take style which bears witness to our curiosity about the relationship between film images and filmed objects in a way which would have excited André Bazin.

▶ Why do so many of the most famous realist films revolve around tiny, apparently insignificant, events? Do films have to be about great achievers and earth-shattering events? What do the dramatic events and changes depicted in Hollywood movies reveal about these films? ●

## Realisms of the 1990s

In March 1995 a group of Danish directors signed a manifesto which they hoped would change cinema. The 'Dogme 95' collective drafted a 'Vow of Chastity' to counter what they saw as illusionary and inauthentic aesthetics propagated by Hollywood and its imitators, and to reinstall film's ability to capture real experience. Written by directors Lars von Trier and Thomas Vinterberg, the Dogme rules recommended that film-makers derive their films out of the

▶ What are your thoughts about the Dogme rules? ●

*Scene from* Festen

circumstances and conditions on the spot where the film is shot, and to play down the influence of the director. Refraining from any affectation of style and personal taste, the Dogme signatories were against the idea that the director was an artist. Thus Dogme precepts challenged an assumption that had underpinned European and American film-making for more than thirty years. By banning any optical work and genre conventions, and insisting on a hand-held camera, they sought an antidote to Hollywood spectacle. By banning director credits, setting films in the here and now, and shooting only in colour, they challenged European auteur and heritage cinema, and American indie aesthetics.

Perhaps the best example of this new spirit was Vinterberg's *Festen* (*The Celebration*, 1998), which was shot on video on location and blown up to 35mm for exhibition. Relating the story of a patrician family gathering at which the son makes allegations of childhood sexual abuse against his father, the film was shot with a hand-held camera in a ceaselessly inquisitive fashion appropriate to both the Dogme aesthetic and the drama's revelatory project. Discussing his film, Vinterberg stressed how the new aesthetic constituted an attempt to get around logistical problems such as poor available light, inappropriate props and traditional acting habits, and to make these work for the film. *Festen*'s immediacy seems to bear out this close interface between film and experience. Dramatically and metaphorically representing the rebellion of one generation against another, *Festen* is the most recent and well-publicized attempt to reinvent cinema according to the realist Lumière model. But while Dogme 95 remained symptomatic of a widespread tendency as the cinema moved into its second century, the movement itself gave rise to few notable films and met with critical scepticism, not least from the eminent British film journal *Sight and Sound*.

The American independent film-making sector sought to represent ordinary American lives. Conventionally seen to have 'happened' with the success of *sex, lies and videotape* (Steven Soderbergh, 1989) at the Sundance Film Festival, a venue designed to promote alternative American 'voices', the indie movie was another episode in the auteurist assumption underpinning modern film culture. Attempting to get back to basics after years of special effects-driven Hollywood 'high concept' blockbusters, the indie movie was to revolve around script and character. *sex, lies and videotape* was essentially a morality tale about a modern marriage destroyed by private and public hypocrisy. Focusing on the confrontation between a conventional yuppie couple and an outsider with highly individual attitudes and sexual predilections, Soderbergh interrogates the 'Greed Is Good' culture advertised in mainstream product such as *Wall Street* (Oliver Stone, 1987) and *Working Girl* (Mike Nichols, 1988). Richard Linklater's *Slacker* was a documentary-style tribute to small town American eccentrics. Like *Clerks*, it celebrates a bunch of oddballs – a man obsessed with parallel worlds, a woman hawking Madonna's cervical smear – and makes a virtue of aimless dialogue and storylines, leaving these to structure the narrative. Other films and auteurs followed.

Reliant upon 'quirky' talk and marketed as personal vision, indie realism has laid itself open to the charge of excessive talkativeness and overly singular quirkiness. Nevertheless, its commitment to other American lives and microcultures has made for some effective replies to the homogenizing technologies and star turns of Hollywood. Indeed, in 1998 a film with all the grainy *vérité* hallmarks of the new DV realism appeared and took in excess of $100 million at the box office. *The Blair Witch Project* (Daniel Myrick & Eduardo Sánchez, 1999) is probably the most notorious, and ingenious, realist film in decades. Shot digitally and edited on a computer for around $25,000, the film was marketed via a website claiming to tell a true

The Blair Witch Project: *the truth is out there . . .*

The Blair Witch Project *probably comes nearest to the Dogme 95 ideal. It was shot on location, with sound produced with the image. Myrick and Sanchez used a hand-held camera, and the film was shot in colour, using no optical work. There was no superficial action, and the film was set in the here and now. It was free of genre trappings, and exhibited on an Academy ratio screen.*

story of three film students who hiked into remote woods in Maryland to make a documentary and were never seen again. Describing itself in the credits as their footage, found months after their disappearance, *The Blair Witch Project* begins as a meticulously recorded account of research, preparations and journey, and ends as the jittery angst-ridden record of people becoming psychologically and physically deranged. Genuinely scared by crew members seeking to heighten the realism, the students abandon the map which seems to tell them nothing, go round and round in circles, and end up at a house where the camera is apparently knocked to the ground and the tape runs out. Because the line between contrivance and experience constantly shifts in *The Blair Witch Project*, we never quite know how knowing or how unnerved these people really are. As a result, even the most sceptical in the audience begin to think there is more to what they are seeing. Of all the films we have looked at which play with the boundary between fiction and truth, this is the eeriest, perhaps even the most consequential.

As with all developments beyond its committee rooms, Hollywood did take note of what was happening in the indie sector. Not only do many of the major studios now have subsidiaries catering to this branch of arthouse exhibition, but also films such as *Magnolia* (Paul Thomas Anderson, 1999) find the studios bringing an indie sensibility to an all-star vehicle, in this case one starring Tom Cruise.

The year 2000 saw another experiment that further pushed out the boundaries of representation. Made within a mainstream context for Hollywood major Sony Pictures, *Timecode* (Mike Figgis) used four DV cameras run on a common timecode and shot in one continuous 93-minute take. Following the private and public lives of an assortment of Hollywood types, *Timecode* was exhibited on a screen split into four separate images. Improvised and employing no script, the film invites you to make sense of what is going on as your attention cuts from frame to frame, in some of which the cameras are obviously inches apart. Like such Hollywood stories as *The Player* (Robert Altman, 1992), *Short Cuts* (Robert Altman, 1993) and *Magnolia*, *Timecode* and *The Blair Witch Project* hark back to cinema's earliest vocation, a peepshow offering unrivalled access to people's lives. As *Big*

*'I happened to mention the idea to the head of Sony Pictures and he said, "We would be interested." Actually, the main interest for them would be that the cost would be the equivalent of the coffee budget on a feature film. And they've now made their digital film and can go back to the real business of kicking scripts to death.' (Figgis on Timecode in conversation with the author, 2000)*

*Brother* showed in the summer of 2000, this candid-camera aesthetic proved irresistible to film-makers and audiences as the cinema entered its second century.

## Mockumentary

The term 'mockumentary' was first used by the American trade paper *Variety* to describe a style of film which gained in popularity in the 1990s, although it was not without precedent. Essentially, the mockumentary, or 'faux documentary' (from the French term for 'fake'), is a documentary-style film in which contrived events and individuals are depicted as though they are real. Employing the conventions of documentary – voice-over, real locations, interviews, archive footage – but in the service of a false premise, mockumentaries play with that contract between the bona fide documentary and its spectator which stipulates that what they are watching is genuine. The mockumentary draws attention to both the fabricated nature of all films, documentaries included, and the fallibility of the spectator, wishing to believe in the veracity of films in general and documentaries in particular. No other genre illustrates the play of aesthetics and experience quite as knowingly as the mockumentary does.

As we have seen, perhaps the most notorious trick played on audiences in recent years was *The Blair Witch Project*, a film built on a conceit that was at least as clever as the accomplishment of audience participation and horror. *This Is Spinal Tap* (Rob Reiner, 1983) was what many regard as the high point of mockumentary, and hit all the right notes in its send-up of heavy metal culture and the band tour documentary. Bathed in thudding metal basslines, this was a *vérité* account of a rock band's comeback amid believably inflated egos, personal tensions and tragic (and hilarious) demises. *Man Bites Dog* (*C'est arrivé près de chez vous*, Rémy Belvaux, André Bonzel & Benoît Poelvoorde, 1992) followed the documentary crew as they filmed the progress of a serial killer so charming that they, and we, end up liking him and become complicit in his dreadful acts. *Man Bites Dog* appeared as the 1990s British debate about screen violence was in full swing, and few films have made audiences focus on the ethics of witnessing screen violence with such uncomfortable results. The mockumentary has distinguished

*Scene from* The Matrix

forebears. *Citizen Kane* (Orson Welles, 1941) was based around a fake newsreel of a fictitious media magnate. When a journalist is asked to investigate Charles Foster Kane by interviewing those who knew him, a far more complex portrait emerges than the bland newsreel 'life'. Making an issue of the believability of the newsreel, and the elusiveness of all truth, *Citizen Kane*, a film repeatedly voted the greatest of all time in *Sight and Sound* magazine and elsewhere, brilliantly draws attention to the artifice of aesthetics.

The documentary tradition, with its real bystanders and concealed cameras, has for decades epitomized unmediated realism for audiences. Part of the reason why the closing years of cinema's first century were so exciting was that high concept Hollywood films and DV experiments both raise issues of cinematic realism, albeit in different ways. Arguably, the hyperrealism of projects such as the *Matrix* films and *Waking Life* (Richard Linklater, 2001) generated downscale reaction. If *The Matrix* (Andy & Larry Wachowski, 1999) undermines consensual reality in favour of mental illusion, it produces pure consciousness rather than consciousness of something. Sitting in the multiplex amid the barrage of image and sound, we perceive through nerve endings via sensation, colour, sound, movement and texture. Our minds and bodies are melded in a simultaneous process of perception as *perception*. By contrast, the real thing in itself, the object or experience that's out there in the world, has become fetishized in works such as *The Blair Witch Project* and *Timecode*, a radical aesthetic that is as much 'different' as it is real. What these films promised was the real as an extra marketing feature. As always, the real is a matter of competing aesthetics. Whenever you point a camera, you turn experience into aesthetic.

# 6. Realism in British Film and Television

*Realist aesthetics have been crucial to film and television in Britain, informing their separate evolutions and forming the basis for their interactions. Realism has provided a mirror for Britain's transition from a white imperial power into a society of vibrant multicultural diversity. Chapter 6 offers an overview of realist currents in British cinema and in television genres ranging from documentary to comedy.*

## The British New Wave

Appearing at a moment of change in world cinema, the British New Wave of the 1960s chimed with attempts to push out the boundaries of representation then being practised in Hollywood, and with bolder European attempts at cinemas of personal expression. As in Hollywood in the late 1950s, the New Wave is associated with the representation of social rebellion and sex. Drawing upon earlier traditions of realism in British cinema such as documentary, the Ealing comedy of the 1940s, and Free Cinema, the New Wave also anticipated the shift from an apparently unmediated record of experience seen in Italian neo-realism, to the complex imagery of subsequent European and American film-making.

Historically, the British New Wave is closely associated with the documentary film-makers of the Free Cinema initiative. We shall look in more detail at this development later, but Free Cinema and the New Wave both sought ways of developing a cinema beyond the boundaries of the commercial mainstream. While studio film-making has

► Social rebellion and sex, teenagers and women … there seems to be a theme running through the evolution of postwar cinema in Hollywood and Britain. Do you think that the lives of teenagers and women are better represented now? ●

► Watching other films starring Albert Finney or Rita Tushingham, to what extent do you think these actors conform to a particular star image? Watching more recent films, then returning to their earlier work, how far are you influenced by the fact that you are watching 'Albert Finney', as opposed to a Nottingham factory worker? ●

► When we talk about the New York locations of *One Fine Day* and the Nottingham locations of *Saturday Night and Sunday Morning*, are we talking about the same kind of location shooting? ●

traditionally been centred in and around London, and British films had traditionally privileged the lives of middle-class, mainly southern characters, the emphasis of the new sensibility was on regional locations and ordinary people.

Setting up financing and production arrangements associated but separate from mainstream production houses, New Wave film-makers such as Karel Reisz, Tony Richardson and Jack Clayton set out to tackle content considered risky at the time. Their films would deal with topics such as prostitution, abortion, homosexuality, alienation and relationship problems. Here were factory workers, office underlings, dissatisfied wives, pregnant girlfriends, runaways, the angry, marginalized, poor and depressed. For the first time, the main characters spoke with regional accents and did things not because they were the done thing, but because experience pushed them in that direction. For the first time, characters in British films lived in streets audiences recognized in towns they knew. *Saturday Night and Sunday Morning* (Karel Reisz, 1960) revolves around a Nottingham factory worker who lives for the weekend. The dialogue has all the brusque authenticity of its Midlands setting. Inspired by a vital realist literature, these films featured a new generation of actors, including Albert Finney, Alan Bates, Rachel Roberts and Rita Tushingham, who had emerged out of regional theatre.

Stylistically, the New Wave directors owed much to British documentarist Humphrey Jennings. Jennings advocated a poetic use of documentary in which film could be used not simply to record reality, but also to interpret what the camera saw in a creative way. What Jennings and the New Wave directors have in common is not a quantifiable world with everything in its place, but a cinema which draws out existential truths underlying day-to-day experience everywhere. In this respect, British New Wave film-makers anticipated the philosophical outlooks animating 1960s Continental arthouse cinema.

In order to catch everyday experience but also tap into hidden meanings, a number of devices were employed. For example, places are used not simply as settings for a fictional narrative, but for themselves. Shots of particular townscapes and landscapes crop up often in these films, suggesting that this narrative is unfolding in a particular town or city, and not just anywhere. In order to humanize the image, to integrate it into a story of universal social truth, as it were, academic Andrew Higson interprets the shot as one indirectly related to the perspectives of the protagonist. In *Saturday Night and Sunday Morning*, for example, we see Arthur and Brenda meeting in a spot overlooking the factory chimneys of Nottingham. Later we see Arthur and Doreen walking in a field overlooking a new housing estate. Because these characters are always already located amid these milieux, their stories seem to arise out of these places. Sequences of shots of urban scenes – cobbled streets, pubs, factory chimneys, dank canals – provide moments where we pause and reflect upon a record of Britain at a particular moment, and an expression of something of the way life is for real people.

The impetus for the New Wave was the literature of the era's 'angry young men', a generation railing against the thwarted hopes and what were seen as the diminished prospects for the postwar world. This emphasis on male experience and its discontents is aesthetically and ideologically significant. New Wave films were preoccupied with the decline of British working-class culture and the traditional model of masculinity which went with it. A chief appeal of these films when they appeared was their unabashed treatment of sex at a time when Victorian attitudes still dominated most households. It was only in 1951 that the X certificate, forerunner of the 18, was put in place by the BBFC.

The 'poetic' treatment of experience to be found in New Wave films links them with the experimental impulse of the French New Wave, the playfulness of which they often mimicked. Arguably, the British films saw male directors with modern outlooks making films about young men with modern outlooks. But such perspectives limit a film's purchase on experience. Echoing the directors' individual takes on contemporary life, the male characters in many New Wave films dominate these perspectives on British experience.

If the neo-realist tone of dutiful revelation lent Italian films an overall sympathy for beleaguered humanity, British New Wave directors depicted a world of men and women at war with each other. Writing about *A Kind of Loving* (John Schlesinger, 1962), critic Penelope Gilliat detected a deep-

▶ Watching *Saturday Night and Sunday Morning*, can you identify other devices that contribute to a sense of real experience unfolding? ●

*Scene from* Saturday Night and Sunday Morning

► What similarities, if any, do you see between the depiction of women in *Saturday Night and Sunday Morning* and the depiction of women in Kevin Smith's *Clerks* (1994)? ●

► Do you think that women receive a better deal in contemporary British films? What passes as complexity in more recent representation of British women? ●

seated misogyny in the plays and books on which New Wave films were based. In war work during the 1940s, British women achieved a measure of economic freedom. But the 1950s saw a backlash and the retrenchment of old ideas about a woman's place.

For all their apparent liberality of representation, the New Wave films were actually deeply conformist, depicting women either as wives and mothers, or as lovers and mistresses. Women were seldom depicted as characters with their own agendas defined independently of men. Arthur in *Saturday Night and Sunday Morning* is torn between the nice, respectable Doreen and the passionate and adulterous Brenda. When we first see Doreen she is a nicely dressed girl at the bar buying crisps for her mum. Going to the pictures with Arthur, she refuses to sit at the back. Back at her mum's after a date, the couple must trick her mum before having sex on the sofa. When we first see Brenda she is out for the evening with Arthur dressed in a short-sleeved blouse and wearing bangles on her wrist, archetypal code since the early days of Hollywood for a woman of low morals. In the scene in which Brenda's husband finds her at the fair with Arthur, he slaps her in public. It is a shocking scene in which you are reminded of your embarrassment at witnessing a violent domestic dispute in public.

Women in these films are associated with domestic spaces – Doreen talks wistfully of having a new house on an estate. Men occupy public spaces – in the final scene, Arthur lobs a stone over a housing estate. While men are active in the world, women 'belong' at home. While men are breadwinners, women are consumers. Brenda represents a woman's struggle against hypocrisy and prejudice. Doreen represents conformity and a comfortable life. Coupled with their limiting perspectives on complex social issues, the gender politics in New Wave films severely limit their ability to represent the reality of postwar British life. Subsequent British realisms are marked by an increasing ability to represent experience, and the increasing identification of realism with arthouse cinema.

## The 1980s

Despite financial problems that had afflicted the British cinema since the late 1960s, British film-making in the early 1980s witnessed something of a realist renaissance characterized by an extension of issues tackled and more emphasis on political comment.

Dominating the early part of the decade was the new political and economic order introduced under Prime Minister Margaret Thatcher. In 1979 a Conservative government came to power with a social programme more radical than seen for generations. The government transformed British welfare provision from a universal cure-all for social ills into one system for those who could afford it and another for those who could not, altering for ever our perceptions of state intervention in the life of the individual. Thatcherism stood for rugged self-determination, materialism, a return to Victorian values, and a crackdown on those who would not conform. From now on, Britons would have to stand on their own two feet. The prevailing ethos encouraged unstinting initiative and adaptability, a forerunner of the 'transferrable skills' workplace culture of today. The 1980s also saw the decline of traditional manufacturing industry, the widespread closure of factories and the rise of IT and service industries. This led to unemployment in the north and in Scotland and Wales, while the south-east and London witnessed an economic boom. To a younger generation unable to find work in an increasingly multicultural but divided Britain, Thatcherism was moralistic and oppressive. Working-class solidarity and community spirit were becoming a thing of the past, as binding legislation made trade unions weak. Young people sought expression in vibrant cultures centred on music and fashion and, briefly, a realist cinema in which the implications of rugged individualism were played out.

The inauguration of Channel 4 in 1982 was a crucial attempt to find and cultivate a cinema audience for British realism. Channel 4's remit was to appeal to minority groups and the unrepresented in British society. Conceived as a publisher-broadcaster rather than, as the BBC and ITV were, a producer-broadcaster, Channel 4 commissioned work from independent production companies. This patronage resulted in a series of low- to medium-budget films that played in

*Cultural critic Judith Williamson's review collection Deadline at Dawn vividly illustrated the implications of trying to represent minority experience in British films during the 1980s.*

▶ Do you think it is possible to change the way people think about social reality by making 'protest' films? Why? Can you think of a contemporary director who does so? ●

cinemas for a time, generating publicity for later TV transmission. Between 1981 and 1990, Channel 4 partially funded 170 features. While few got theatrical exposure, some performed well at the box office. Key among them was *My Beautiful Laundrette* (Stephen Frears, 1985) and *Letter to Brezhnev* (Chris Bernard, 1985).

Central to Thatcherism was the assertion of 'family values' to counter what was seen as the moral disintegration of British life in the 1960s. Many of the best British films of the 1980s need to be seen as reassertions of individual and minority experiences in the face of the prevailing moralism. *My Beautiful Laundrette* tells of a young Asian businessman who embraces Thatcherite private enterprise, but is rejected by the white establishment. His relationship with a gay ex-National Front member invited the exploration of the truly complex motives that animate real people's lives. *Letter to Brezhnev* found two young women in search of relief from the drudgery of factory life in contemporary Liverpool. *High Hopes* (Mike Leigh, 1988) and *Life Is Sweet* (Leigh, 1990) traced the fates of ordinary Britons as they attempted to negotiate a way to live in Thatcher's Britain.

Reflecting the attrition of community, 1980s realism was less a call for collective action than a series of ripostes against the established order. Protest rather than action characterized British realism during this era. Its film-makers did not belong to a movement with a manifesto or a set of aims as the Free Cinema or New Wave directors had. There was no 1980s style as there had been a 1960s style. What stands out as we look back are particular films, particular interactions.

## Ken Loach and Mike Leigh

For their sustained and articulate critiques of Thatcherism, two directors stand out. Both legatees of BBC-sponsored drama of the 1960s and 1970s, while Ken Loach followed the New Wave impulse to reconcile documentary portraits of economically ravaged Britain with depictions of its pitiful victims, Mike Leigh focused on the impact of decline on individuals and their families. The aesthetic which Loach honed in BBC dramas such as *Cathy Come Home* (1966) and *Days of Hope* (1975) was extended and refined in a series of films dealing with the legacy of Thatcherism. As a committed socialist, Loach was actually unable to work during the conservative 1980s. *Raining Stones* (1993) focuses on a Lancashire family and their struggle to make ends meet. Bob is determined that his daughter will have a white dress for her first Holy Communion. His attempt to make it happen brings home the diminished opportunities that afflict millions of the unemployed in one of Loach's most tough-minded but funny films. In *Ladybird Ladybird* (1994), Maggie is a 'problem parent', a loud-mouthed mother hounded by the social services and doomed to a series of difficult relationships. Then she meets the gentle Jorge and it seems as if she can start again. Loach deals in strong emotions and audience identification, characteristics we tend to associate with Hollywood melodrama, shaped by wide shots, long takes, naturalistic acting and the looser exposition of documentary. Locating identifiable feelings in an identifiable Britain lends Loach's films the apparent patina of everyday working life.

Mike Leigh's work also embodies loose structure and an unobtrusive use of camerawork and editing. But here the emphasis is on a survey of personality and familial and social interactions. Early work such as the BBC TV plays *Abigail's Party* (1976) and *Nuts in May* (1977) retained a focus on embarrassing dynamics which could be excruciating to sit through! Not that the plays were bad, but by taking the observation of manners to such a pitch Leigh tapped into British conventions of behaviour and attitude that are widely shared if seldom acknowledged. Focusing on families and close friends in enclosed settings adds to the claustrophobia. Often described by critics as 'social surrealism' after that art movement which represented reality in exaggerated style, Leigh's work has been criticized for its apparent celebration of personal tics and mannerisms. But few British film-makers caught the times more succinctly. Of *Career Girls* (1997), critic Stella Bruzzi wrote in *Sight and Sound*: 'Mike Leigh is to fiction film what the best *cinéma-vérité* filmmakers are to documentary: an acute observer of nuance who constructs drama out of incidental events we would otherwise not notice at all.'

*Life Is Sweet* (1990) measured the dreams of Enfield suburbanites against the rhetoric of Thatcherite private enterprise. Andy wants to start his own business from a filthy mobile snack bar. Aubrey wants to bring nouvelle cuisine to north London. Neither really knows what he's doing, while

Life Is Sweet: *Wendy's daughters Nicola and Nathalie muddle through*

Andy's wife, Wendy, struggles to keep the family smiling whatever. In *Secrets and Lies* (1996) black optometrist Hortense wants to find out who her mother is. Factory worker Cynthia feels lonely and unloved. As her daughter Roxanne's twenty-first birthday approaches, the scene is set for some painful truths. Leigh's most commercially successful film and a winner at the Oscars, *Secrets and Lies* interrogated the yawning distances between family members and racial minorities wrought by divisive Thatcherite policies. Ironically, one summer after its release, that symbol of British philanthropy Diana Spencer died in a car accident, prompting widespread and public British mourning. The same year, New Labour had been elected with a massive majority, pledging itself to a new and inclusive social consensus in Britain.

## Since 1990

The precarious funding environment that had begun to set in during the 1980s was exacerbated by the Broadcasting Act of 1990. This made Channel 4 responsible for raising its own advertising revenue. The result was significantly less money for investment in film projects. But spurred by a number of institutional and cultural incentives, the late 1990s saw another renaissance in British cinema.

British film-making has perennially been faced with the decision either to emulate Hollywood models or to come up with a homegrown alternative. *Four Weddings and a Funeral* (Mike Newell, 1994) and *The Full Monty* (Peter Cattaneo, 1997) best exemplify the different approaches taken to this problem. *Four Weddings* was a romantic comedy set in the Home Counties stockbroker belt and starring Hugh Grant and American import Andie MacDowell. Appealing to a pre-Thatcherite England of castles, country inns and tea on the lawn, the film was a huge success in America (spurred by MacDowell's starring role), and the middle-class Middle English occasional filmgoer attracted to its literate examination of English manners. Co-produced by prominent 1990s production company Polygram with Channel 4, *Four Weddings* epitomized the cautious commercial formula on which British cinema was banking.

*Scene from* The Fully Monty

*The Full Monty* was another huge success. However, developed by Channel 4 but produced by 20th Century Fox, ironically its profits ended up in America. The conceit in which unemployed Sheffield welders regain a sense of dignity by becoming male strippers in a working men's club rejuvenated the theme of disenchanted masculinity which animated New Wave cinema. *The Full Monty*'s nostalgia for working-class community became a running theme in what journalists described as 'Britflicks', small quirky stories with big popular appeal. I term such films as *The Full Monty*, *Brassed Off* (Mark Herman, 1996) and *Billy Elliot* (Stephen Daldry, 2000) 'triumph-over-adversity narratives', as they revolve around ordinary, usually male Britons rising above economic strife with unexpected prowess. Yet, structured tightly around a Hollywood-style narrative formula, such solutions as these films offer feel like blind optimism in the face of sociopolitical complexity. Indeed, the triumph-over-adversity formula might be regarded as a metaphor for a plucky little homegrown industry pitching against the Goliath of American competition. Its ideological bent found *The Full Monty* championed by the incoming Labour government of Tony Blair for its 'Cool Britannia' credibility. These films also displayed something of the hostility towards women that we find in the New Wave films. Revolving around men's problems and resolutions, female characters are invariably defined by their relationships with male characters. Another current is the work of Jamie Thraves. Trading in neither the angry grit of Ken Loach nor the triumph-against-

▶ Neo-realism, Iranian cinema, the 'Britflick': why is it so many realist films are triumph-over-adversity narratives? ●

▶ What should a 'typically British' film seek to do? ●

adversity narrative, *The Low Down* (2000) set a freewheeling and humorous story of friendship, betrayal and romantic diffidence among a set of twenty-somethings in north London.

Should British cinema be a social realist cinema true to Britain's esteemed documentary heritage? Or should it come into its own in another guise? The triumph-over-adversity cycle was an attempt to compete with Hollywood by situating a Hollywood-style feelgood formula in a British setting. It is interesting to compare Mike Leigh, widely thought of as having a typically 'British' style, with the typical Hollywood realism of *One Fine Day*. With its loose structure, unobtrusive camerawork and editing, Leigh couldn't seem further from the tight narrative, functional camerawork and editing, and resolved political story of *One Fine Day*. *Career Girls* may revolve around a pair of smart young college-educated professionals not unlike Melanie Parker, but it crucially charts their lazy weekend as opposed to a high-achieving busy week. However, in among the leisurely shapelessness, there lies a minute examination of ordinary men and women and their familial and social interactions. By comparison, the characters in *One Fine Day* seem more like a screenwriter's 'types', with archetypal interactions and tensions. There may be no 'political' storyline to resolve in Leigh as there is in *One Fine Day*, but cumulatively you sense that what you have seen is entirely symptomatic of the British status quo.

Yet there were film-makers working in the 1990s whose work engaged with real experience and with aesthetics in original ways. If Britflicks offered uncomplicated stories of dreams realized and hardship overcome, directors such as Carine Adler, Shane Meadows, Lynne Ramsay and Pawel Pawlikowski brought ambiguity into depictions of British life. Co-produced by the British Film Institute and Channel 4, Adler's *Under the Skin* (1997) relates an angry and grief-stricken young woman's response to the death of her mother against the backdrop of the housing estates and clubs of contemporary Merseyside. Shane Meadows's *TwentyFourSeven* (1997) seemed to parody the triumph-over-adversity film with a seedy sporting coach's failed attempt to inject purpose into the disaffected youth of a Nottingham suburb. Veering between comedy and darkness in Mike Leigh fashion, *A Room for Romeo Brass* (1999) charts the friendships between a black Nottingham schoolboy, his sickly friend next door, and a dangerous social misfit. After the misogyny of the New Wave and subsequent examinations of damaged British manhood, Meadows's take on male humiliation was textured and complex. Another close-up study of youth, Ramsay's *Ratcatcher* (1999), was set in a Glasgow tenement during a refuse strike in the mid 1970s. Haunted by his involvement in a friend's drowning, a young boy retreats into a fantasy world, the film delicately teetering between the dirty realism outside and the sense it makes to those who have to live with it. Produced by BBC Films, Pawlikowski's *Last Resort* (2000) was a telling portrait of what Britain became in the final decades of the century as a young Russian woman is detained and exploited as she works in webcam pornography while awaiting political asylum.

*Scene from* Ratcatcher

Hyped as yet another renaissance in British cinema's fortunes, the year 2002 saw the appearance of strong works from Loach (*Sweet Sixteen*), Leigh (*All or Nothing*) and Ramsay (*Morvern Callar*). For their rich and ambiguous relationships between experience, narrative and subjectivity, these films demonstrate that a viable British realist cinema is still out there.

## Realism and British television

Television is integral to the audiovisual landscape of contemporary British life. Switched on in the morning, breakfast television provides the backdrop to preparations for the day ahead, enabling a connection between the private lives from which we emerge to go to school or work, and the society to which we belong. There in the afternoon when school finishes, there in the evening when work finishes, television brings social, political and cultural commentary, other people's lives, into our lives until it is switched off at the end of the day. A link with the Britain outside our homes, television informs and shapes our perception of society and our place within it. Broadcasting while we engage in a multitude of activities around it, television is essential to the texture of everyday life. Many get their perspectives on the world around them largely from television.

### News and current affairs

While television may reflect the society we live in, we should be as careful when we see the TV set as a window on the world

▶ What kind of compromises do you think might be made with the truth by CNN, or a Hollywood studio when making action films? ●

as we are when talking about films in these terms. Ideally, objectivity and independence are essential to TV news and current affairs. The 'stories' that appear as items on the TV news are most likely to be considered to be true. But should they be? News coverage is as aesthetically and ideologically managed as the most 'realistic' Hollywood film. Conversely, the global news service CNN often provides the 'factual' backdrop to Hollywood films such as *Contact* (Robert Zemeckis, 1997), lending the cinemagoer the impression that news is actually breaking, which adds veracity to the fictional film. CNN's worldwide reach has made it one of the most respected news agencies, its logo instantly recognizable. As we know, product placement is integral to many Hollywood films.

News and current affairs programmes constitute a genre with conventions and parameters that are as rigorously observed as those of a romantic comedy, thriller or TV drama. Of all the TV genres, you would think that the news embodies the most immediate interface with day-to-day experience imaginable. But if you know how to watch the news, its formats and biases will become increasingly obvious and readable. While the ongoing world experience may consist of real events and developments, the formats and biases in which it reaches you are the result of procedures of editorial evaluation which transform raw experience into easily digestible news items. News items fall into particular topics – crime, disasters, sport, accidents, politics, the arts – each news programme featuring two or more of these topics. Imagine how much of the sheer mass of activities undertaken during one day across the world either cannot be categorized or is insignificant, and it will give you some idea of how bias is built into news coverage, even in the early stages of evaluation. Masses and masses of events and developments in people's private lives never find their way into the news because they are not deemed newsworthy. What TV news gives us is the 'big picture'. To be newsworthy, a story must be significant to a lot of people. It must also fit the topic-driven format of a news programme.

To study news programmes closely is to witness how bias works in the way stories are presented. The language used, the visuals used, where a particular story comes in a programme's sequence of items, the length of an item – all help to shape the programme's take on experience. Point-of-view introduces bias into reportage. Ask yourself what might have been left out. By stressing that *10,000* firemen's jobs may be lost as an outcome of their pay dispute, a programme implicitly criticizes the seeming recklessness of the firemen involved in the dispute. Notice how representatives of officialdom tend to be seen as professionals in professional settings. The General Secretary of the Fire Brigades Union is filmed among fellow strikers, whereas the government minister in charge of fire services is filmed against the backdrop of the Houses of Parliament. Notice, too, how the position of the story in the newscast confers significance. In autumn 2002 the firemen's strike was top of the newscast before being usurped by strikes elsewhere as discontent seemed to spread to other areas of the public sector. Meanwhile, responding, you might argue, to public and media apathy about the moral legitimacy of the Church in British society, an item on a child abuse scandal involving a Catholic priest was lower on the agenda. Amusing items tend to be shorter, inserted as entertaining diversions such as one in which an animated cartoon was censored for asking: 'Is George Bush a moron?' Arguably, this brevity makes it impossible to tackle the thornier issue of why such a question might be asked at a time of possible US-sponsored war with Iraq.

There are a number of institutional issues that make for biased reporting. As reporters as a matter of course make the rounds of the police, the courts and parliament, the stories they glean tend to receive priority coverage. Accessibility and strong visuals influence the editing of the news. Another issue is 'common sense'. Society will tolerate certain stories, but not those that challenge widespread perceptions of what is sensible or morally acceptable. As Britain's primary channel of public information, the BBC has a stake in promoting a particular consensus around content and style of reportage. Conversely, CNN and Rupert Murdoch's Sky News are shaped by a profit-making agenda. Time and the 'sound bite' culture tend to militate against the fuller exploration of issues on the news. Complex causes and effects become reduced to attention-grabbing headlines and visuals. Conflict, whether between countries, political factions and the state, or government and the unions, makes easily digestible and watchable news so tends to shape coverage. All these instances of bias interact with journalistic ideals of fairness and balance, introducing such ideological preferences as interfere with the objective representation of the news.

Gender also plays a role in this representation. At the centre of the news programme is the newsreader, invariably a man. Serious, authoritative but viewer-friendly, the newsreader marshals journalists, often women, from locations around the world, cueing them to deliver their reports. The fact that newsreaders tend to be male has ideological implications. Supposedly bringing a rational and unemotional tenor to the programme, the newsreader puts stories in context. He appears to have an overall view of the events and issues arising out of events. In shows such as *Channel 4 News* and BBC2's *Newsnight*, Jon Snow and Jeremy Paxman go to the underlying issues, aggressively pursuing them in studio interviews and debates. Anchored by these intelligent and conscientious figures, these programmes instill confidence in viewers requiring insightful and rigorous news coverage.

There is no reason, of course, why a woman cannot bring an informed, unemotional and aggressive style to newsreading, interviewing and analysis, and increasingly women are reading the news on Channels 4 and 5 and the BBC. The perception that it is a man's world, men that make the news, and men who should anchor current affairs programmes, is being challenged by a generation of capable women journalists.

Some current affairs programmes have developed an investigative function. *Newsnight* investigated the plight of British Muslims detained by the US authorities at Guantanamo Bay in Cuba. By following a solicitor's campaign to prove their innocence, this item elicited popular credibility and viewer sympathy for a West Midlands family. Drawing upon interviews with family members and Pentagon officials, the report generated the impression of a crusade on behalf of ordinary people like you and me, connecting with real audiences as well as generating a dramatic sense of breaking news.

Like any other TV programme, the news must entertain. Dramatic reconstructions, slow-motion archive footage – all are used for aesthetic impact. To gauge public opinion on the issue of possible British involvement in war with Iraq, 'The Propaganda War' slot introduced by *Channel 4 News* in

▶ For a spell in the summer of 2004, two women dominated the news in Britain. One, Faria Alam, for her affair with the manager of the English national football team Sven-Goran Erikson; the other, Nadia Almada, for becoming the unexpected winner on *Big Brother*. Why did these women's stories loom so large in the media? ●

2003 employed stop-motion photography and acted-out interviews. Unfortunately, coming halfway through the programme and lasting only around twenty minutes, its aesthetic impact was greater than the impact of the discussion that was its purpose. The result did little more than prompt the viewer to consider the issue as one they should be thinking about. On BBC1's *Question Time*, rhetoric is highly prized, the programme pausing every few minutes while the audience applauds a point well put.

The relationship between the reporting of events and the shaping of popular opinion is crucially at stake in TV news coverage. You have only to consider how many news providers are out there to realize the extent to which our perceptions of day-to-day events across the world are products of the way in which we are told what we are told.

## Documentary

The term 'documentary' is derived from the French word *documentaire*, meaning a travelogue or illustrated lecture. The earliest documentaries are the non-fiction *actualités* of the Lumière brothers that we looked at in Chapter 1. We tend to think of the documentary as a guided tour through some aspect of real experience. The classic TV documentary format used in *Horizon* or the 1970s series *World at War*, for example, falls into this expository mode, descending from the purpose and aesthetics of the documentary movement in British cinema of the 1930s.

Theorist and film-maker John Grierson is usually credited with having coined the expression 'documentary' in a 1926 review of *Moana* (Robert Flaherty, 1925), a filmed account of the uncorrupted life of Polynesians in the South Pacific. Grierson saw the form as a way of imparting information about the real world and educating the audience, as well as treating filmed experience in a creative way. This dual function of educating and representing resonates with an interaction between experience and aesthetics that has been a running theme throughout this book. In the 1930s the distinction between being informative in a documentary and treating what the camera sees in a creative way was much more clear-cut than it is now. Now we are wiser about how films and TV programmes work, and we accept that film-makers can manipulate representations of experience in many different

Housing Problems: *Do you get a sense of the urgency of this experience?*

*'It may sound extreme, but it is possible to argue that the documentary film has no privileged relation to reality, as both fiction and documentary films employ the same technologies – mechanics, optics and photochemistry.'*
(Warren Buckland, Teach Yourself Film Studies, p. 121)

▶ Do you think that our cynicism about documentary reportage has made us cynical about the world around us? ●

▶ Do you appreciate that propaganda is a discourse, or discourses, designed to propagate a particular doctrine or practice? Perhaps all documentary is propaganda, whether intentional or not. Discuss. ●

ways. Contemporary theorist Bill Nichols has identified a range of types of documentary that recall, in a more nuanced way, the distinction that Grierson was getting at.

The British documentary movement of the 1930s was an expression of widespread official concern that the interests of a democracy were not well served as long as many of its citizens were ill educated. Grierson recognized that film could be a powerful means of informing and educating the British public. Grierson gathered a group of like-minded film-makers around him, overseeing the production of hundreds of short films, some of which remain classics of their kind. *Housing Problems* (Edgar Anstey & Arthur Elton, 1935), *Enough to Eat* (Edgar Anstey, 1936) and *Workers and Jobs* (Arthur Elton, 1935) focused on pressing issues such as urban slums, hunger and unemployment. These films were expository essays that observed and reported these problems using actual footage, spot interviews and explanatory voice-overs. They were the forerunners of the prime-time exposés and current affairs investigations we see every week on television. The key difference is that these films were not the initiatives of an audience-hungry media, and now seem more sober than the sensational programmes of today. In 1935 the government trade organization the Empire Marketing Board announced: 'For the State, the function of official documentary is to win the consent of this new public for the existing order.' The public information remit of the Grierson-inspired documentary has been described as propaganda for a conservative status quo.

An important figure to emerge from the Grierson stable was Humphrey Jennings, whose poetic *Listen to Britain* (1940) and *Fires Were Started* (1943) have made Jennings for many one of the most important British directors. Although closely associated in earlier work with the patronizing flavour of the public information film, Jennings's later work has a feeling for the aesthetic possibilities of the documentary which would remain influential until well into the postwar period. *Listen to Britain* was a chronicle of twenty-four hours in the life, work and music of Britain. Interpreting 'music' in the broadest way, the film incorporated the sounds of labour, machinery, the city and the country, blending these with piano recitals and public concerts. Marrying image and soundtrack, music becomes the aesthetic motor of *Listen to Britain*, thanks to Jennings's co-director and co-editor Stewart McAllister and their sound man Ken Cameron. *Fires Were Started* was a tribute to the firemen who bravely tackled blazes caused by German bombing during the London Blitz of 1940–41. Watching it now, the everyday work of the firemen takes on an epic dimension. Where Jennings departed from Grierson was in believing that the individuals shown in documentaries should never be taken out of the milieux in which they lived and worked, in which the camera found them. Whereas the Grierson project found middle-class film-makers venturing into the slums and alleyways of a social jungle that was thoroughly alien to them and their audiences in search of the 'dignity' of the British worker, Jennings saw him or her always already caught up in ordinary daily circumstances.

By consciously turning raw actual experiences into art, Jennings was acknowledging something which contemporary documentary makers and their audiences take for granted; that film-making is as much artifice as it is actual. Since World War II, British documentary has sought to escape the confines of the public information film and increasingly acknowledged its debt to aesthetics. Jennings's attempt to find music and poetry amid the doings of day-to-day British life resonated in the 1950s with the film-makers of the Free Cinema movement. Writers emerging from the film journal *Sequence* (1947–52), the Free Cinema documentary makers wished to challenge the literary and middle-class pretensions of the postwar British 'quality' feature film, making their vows to a documentary rendition of popular working-class and regional British life. First appearing in a series of programmes at the National Film Theatre between 1956 and 1959, and sufficiently 'alternative' to lend rebellious credibility to the Free Cinema project, *Momma Don't Allow* (Karel Reisz & Tony Richardson, 1956) observed the freewheeling dynamics of a north London jazz club. *Every Day Except Christmas* (Lindsay Anderson, 1957) documented the life of Covent Garden Market. So called because they were free of the financial and aesthetic restraints of mainstream feature film-making, by reintroducing real people into British cinema, the Free Cinema directors looked forward not only to the British New Wave, but also a golden age of TV realism.

Over recent decades, the observational style of documentary associated with Grierson has been superseded

*'Implicit in our attitude is a belief in freedom, in the importance of people and in the significance of the everyday.' (From the Free Cinema manifesto, 1956)*

*Scene from* Momma Don't Allow

Cathy Come Home: *Reg and Cathy, the social specimen as character study*

Nichols is not the only way into documentary. While influential, this categorization is just one way of accounting for documentary practice. Categorizing these films according to institution, genre (e.g. *cinéma-vérité*), gender, ideology and medium (TV versus film documentary) throws other light upon them. It is also worth bearing in mind that most documentaries now tend to be a combination of more than one of Nichols's modes.

by more personal and constructed 'histories'. Strong narratives, point-of-view and distinctive characterization are becoming more pronounced. In 1966 Ken Loach's *Cathy Come Home* mixed real reportage with a dramatic reconstruction using actors and a script. The public information ideals of objectivity and solemn reportage are continually being eroded by new work in the genre. The investigative strand of documentary has become a key feature of television schedules. *Betrayal* (ITV, 1982) found a journalist researching a member of the East German state police. As the programme progressed, it became clear that this man's identity was not what it seemed. Satire has increasingly been used to undermine the staid traditional model. In the Channel 4 series *Brass Eye* (1997–2002) presenter Chris Morris tricked genuine celebrities and experts into believing that this was a bona fide documentary series when it was anything but! We have seen how the mockumentary not only mocks the traditional documentary, but has created a culture of manufactured histories as well.

The rendition of the real on film is always subject to circumstantial and aesthetic factors. Theorist Bill Nichols's modes of documentary form are an attempt to account for the extent to which film-makers play upon these conditions and aesthetics. Though still in a state of revision, for our purposes Nichols's documentary categories are: expository, observational, participatory, reflexive and performative. The expository mode imparts knowledge of the world using a detached 'voice-of-God' commentary, sometimes blended with poetic or romantic inferences about experience. The *Horizon* programme *The Secret of El Dorado* does just this. The work of the documentary movement falls mainly into this category, although Nichols has added a 'poetic' category to account for such films as *Night Mail* (Harry Watt & Basil Wright, 1936). While the expository documentary creates a strong impression of objectivity by using voice-overs and a more educational and informative structure, the poetic mode tends to acknowledge its aesthetics. The observational mode finds the film-makers unobtrusively recording individuals as if they are unaware of being filmed. Lacking a voice-of-God commentary alongside illustrative coherent visuals, this type records events unfolding in real time. The Channel 4 series *The Salon* is a good recent example. The participatory mode involves increasingly interventionist tactics. *Louis Theroux's Weird Weekends* (Bravo, 1997–2002) found Theroux profiling strange or controversial people, living with them and earning their trust. The results have been funny and unsettling! Shown in cinemas, *Bowling for Columbine* (2002) has been a highly successful participatory documentary in which film-maker Michael Moore interviewed key figures in connection with the prevalence of gun-related crime in America. Moore's *Fahrenheit 9/11* (2004) interrogated the Bush administration's post-9/11 'War on Terror' and was a well-publicised and controversial intervention in the political process in an election year. The Channel 4 documentary *Young, Nazi and Proud* is a revealing participatory exposé of a young British National Party candidate. The reflexive mode finds the film-maker going a step further by making more apparent the conventions of representation on which the expository, observational and participatory modes depend. The classic documentary *The Nightcleaners* (1975) opens the whole form of documentary up for examination. Emerging out of the radical 1960s, the collective or film-making co-op tended to be grant-aided, integrating production, distribution and exhibition, and was heavily involved in current debates around representation. The performative mode wilfully draws attention to representational conventions and style in order to demonstrate the limitations and assumptions of conventional documentary discourse. *Feltham Sings* reveals and entertains in equal measure.

Evoking the scale model again, we could place the expository documentary at the Lumière end because it assumes an unproblematic match between what the camera sees and what is to be seen. At the opposite end the Channel 4 documentary *Feltham Sings* evokes the contrived representations of the Méliès fantasy. In between these two extremes lie examples of observational, participatory and reflexive documentaries.

*'… sheds light on the darkest corner of America's soul – and the man with the torch is the unlikely figure of a shuffling, bespectacled and overweight and underpaid film-maker in baggy jeans.'* (Urban Cinefile critic on Michael Moore's Bowling for Columbine, www.urbancinefile.com, 2003)

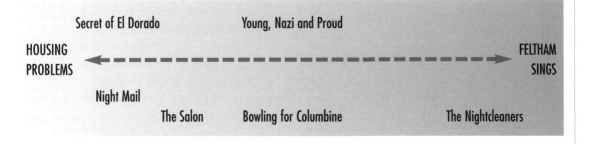

## The expository mode

*Horizon* is a classic series launched in the 1960s and produced by the BBC. Its expository mode is consonant with the public information ethos with which the BBC is associated. *Horizon* manages to explain aspects of the world around us and to show how problems and pitfalls arising out of our environment can be overcome. Expository documentaries combine a voice-of-God commentary dryly relating the facts with poetic flourishes. In T*he Secret of El Dorado* (BBC2, 19 December 2002) we are told how scientists and researchers may have discovered a lost civilization in the Amazon basin in South America. Typically, the expository documentary employs narration in tandem with the visuals as one explains and is reinforced by the other. What you are told becomes what you see, in other words. For instance, here we see footage of a grassy landscape. We are told that this is a savannah crisscrossed with mysterious lines. We then see the landscape bisected with lines. We are told that islands of forest on the savannah contain evidence of an ancient civilization. We see a montage of broken pieces of pottery and tools. Punctuating the account, the narrator reads extracts from historical diaries, and researchers explain the history and their methods and findings straight to camera. Propelled by an air of investigation, we seem to be uncovering and solving this enigma as the experts are.

The rapid montages leaven the factual exposition with elements of poetry, much like the poem makes the daily process of letter delivery more interesting in *Night Mail*. For example, stop-motion photography is used to show clouds passing overhead, a nice way of illustrating the passage of time. We see plants growing at many, many times the natural rate as we are told that the prehistoric civilization turned infertile into fertile land. Every so often there is a 'beauty shot' of the sun setting on the Amazon. As the narrator tells of disease brought by European settlers, indigenous actors simulate death by closing their eyes.

As we have seen, when looking at the work of the British documentary movement, the expository mode is often associated with a progressive political agenda. Here, in *The Secret of El Dorado*, researchers show how soil erosion and poor crop yields are countered by distributing especially rich soil far afield, reproducing its potential and subsequently increasing food production. The programme ends with the promise that the world's food problems could, at least in theory, be cured in this way.

## The observational mode

*The Salon* (2003–), like *Young, Nazi and Proud* and *Feltham Sings*, was commissioned by Channel 4, a broadcaster that airs programmes from independent producers, a strategy that has given Channel 4 its reputation for diversity and experiment. *The Salon* followed the day-to-day business of a south London hair salon from its establishment. As in the 'reality TV' show *Big Brother*, the hidden cameras and microphones capture the staff's activities, off moments and evolving dynamics in real time. Although there is some audience orientation provided by voice-over, the style invites us to speculate and draw our own conclusions about the process of running the salon and the progress of staff relationships. As with documentaries shot in the observational mode, there are no interviews.

The 'staff' of Channel 4's The Salon

Like reality TV, *The Salon* offers apparently full access to the workplace around the clock, overlapping talk, impromptu bits of business and warts included! Eager to make the enterprise work, manager Paul is seen cautioning, lecturing and berating individuals. At one point we saw him playing an 'air guitar' as if momentarily unaware that he's on camera. From time to time, other individuals forget that there is a camera there, looking straight at it in passing. Reality TV and observational documentary collide as we spot individuals adjusting their personal microphones. Juniors mess about in a sunbed cubicle. Without providing full narration as it does in the expository-style documentary, a voice-over will occasionally help to shape what we see into micro-narratives. Ricardo gives Oliver emotional support, for example. Adey bonds with a client. Even in the archetypal observational documentaries produced by Frederick Wiseman in America in the 1960s, you find the material being quietly shaped by the editing and camerawork in order to make certain points about what you are seeing. In *The Salon* it was clear from the earliest programmes that certain individuals were being groomed as 'characters', a tendency suggested in the 'star'-driven credit sequence at the beginning of the show.

### The participatory mode

*Young, Nazi and Proud* (4 November 2002) was a documentary in the *Dispatches Investigation* series which profiled the leader of the British National Party Mark Collett. A participatory documentary, *Young, Nazi and Proud* found the interviewer following Collett into areas of his public political life and his personal life, and increasingly participating in the programme's meaning.

It begins as Mark is seen supporting canvassers as they rally support for the BNP in a forthcoming by-election. We see this well-dressed young man coaching party members and talking to potential voters. Gradually, Mark and the interviewer establish a friendly rapport, the interviewer gaining the trust of Mark's family and hanging out with him in local pubs and clubs. Then the interviewer's voice-over starts expressing his own feelings about the kind of person Collett is. As we see Collett preening himself in the mirror, we are told that 'Mark appeared to think a lot about looking good.' As we see Collett exercising with weights, the interviewer narrates: 'Mark clearly enjoyed being filmed.' While the visuals and the rapport suggest a positive and laddish relationship, the voice-over reveals what the interviewer is really thinking.

Increasingly unguarded disclosures become common as we see Mark in his car, in his flat espousing racist and misogynistic views, his admiration for Hitler and the Nazis. The voice-over tells us that Collett does not realize that he has been filmed talking favourably about Germany under the Nazis. We are told that the interviewer, apparently his friend, is actually of Jewish descent. Finally, pushing Collett as far as he dare, the interviewer confronts him with these revelations. In a chilling and quite excruciating scene, Collett insists on stopping the interview and turning the camera off.

The key aim of the documentary *Young, Nazi and Proud* is to expose Mark Collett's bid for political respectability as a reactionary and dangerous development in contemporary Britain. Initially seeming to us (and to Collett) to be an advertisement for the BNP leader, the documentary surreptitiously reveals Collett to be a strutting egotist with fascist principles. The programme also invites us to speculate about Collett's background. We are told that he failed to fit in at university, and his girlfriend left him because of his political views. We witness how his mother, of both parents the most dominant personality, fusses obsessively over Mark, while sister Amy supports him at party events (reluctantly it turns out) once his girlfriend has gone. At one point, a seemingly objective shot of a clutch of BNP supporters wrapped in Union Jacks appears as the narrator voices his opinion that the BNP is more a cult than a party. This perspective on a dysfunctional family and an isolated sect of extreme opinion is difficult to ignore, recalling as it does the work of Nick Broomfield.

Michael Moore's films mix wry distance, pathos and wit as he interrogates America's most sacred institutions. *Bowling for Columbine* was made in the wake of an incident in which a pair of schoolchildren shot dead several of their classmates in Columbine, Colorado. Employing probing interviews, door-stepping, documentary evidence and embarrassing confrontations, the film is a brave call for common sense in a society in which the gun has become sacred.

### The reflexive mode

Because it foregrounds film techniques and devices rather than appearing like a window through which we witness experience as it happens, the reflexive documentary often has a political or ideological agenda. A film drawing attention to the way in which the world is represented also has the effect of highlighting the representational strategies that we are used to seeing in documentaries.

*The Nightcleaners* is a TV film made in 1975 about women who clean offices after hours and the working conditions they have to endure. Made by the Berwick Street Film Collective, the original idea was to record the campaign to improve the cleaners' lot using interviews, an 'objective' camera, and the methods and stylistics of conventional TV documentary. But as the shoot progressed, the film-makers' growing involvement in the dispute resulted in a film that not only asks questions of society generally, but also questions the traditional passivity of the spectator.

Rather than documenting events in an easy-to-follow order, events are shown in fragments, cutting seems unmotivated, images are repeated or frozen on-screen. Rather than document a typical day at work, the film-makers sought to infuse the working experience with the interrelationships between family life and political activity, the cleaners and the union, working-class cleaners and middle-class leaflet distributors. In this way, these workers and their conditions are shown as participating in a wider sociopolitical fabric, just as all our lives do.

A number of unusual devices are used to serve the film's disruption of the traditionally comfortable relationship between the spectator and the film-maker. By and large, we tend to regard a film as a finished work of art that we sit back and consume. As we have seen, films naturalize certain states of affairs, presenting a world in which problems and contradictions are smoothed out or resolved. Using isolated images, reframing them, replacing the diegetic soundtrack with other sounds, using slow motion to show in detail the methodical drudgery, isolation and boredom the average office cleaner endures, *The Nightcleaners* not only disrupts the traditional rapport between spectator and film, but also comments on wider social inequalities. Perhaps its most powerful message was to show the discrepancy between the idealistic talk of contemporary feminism and what real working women had to endure in low-paid jobs. By confronting us with the disruption of traditional aesthetics, *The Nightcleaners* shows how those aesthetics operate to serve the interests of the political establishment.

More recently, the work of Errol Morris in the reflexive mode has attracted growing attention. Co-produced by Channel 4, *Mr Death: The Rise and Fall of Fred A. Leuchter, Jr* (1999) is a compelling portrait of the 'death row technologist' who has spent his life repairing and designing electric chairs, lethal injection apparatus, gas chambers and gallows. When he gets involved with a neo-Nazi, Leuchter travels to the World War II concentration camp at Auschwitz and analyses bricks and mortar so as to prove that the Nazi extermination of the Jews did not happen. Completely without irony or a shred of self-awareness, Leuchter becomes an increasingly pathetic figure. Employing a variety of non-traditional documentary devices, including stylized reconstructions, studio interviews, slow motion and found footage, Morris asks whether this man is evil or simply deluded. But no single event can explain Leuchter.

Undermining *cinéma-vérité*'s traditional documentary verisimilitude, what counts as true arises gradually out of the play of investigative tropes. By continually drawing attention to film as film, Morris shows that truth is something we really cannot fix. We can only explore competing fictions in search of the reality of events.

## The performative mode

*Feltham Sings* (Channel 4, 17 December 2002) is a documentary about the inmates of the Feltham Young Offenders Institution. The experience of serving time behind bars is conveyed by conventional talking heads and informative subtitles, but also via the inmates' songs, the performance of which is shaped by the film itself. This has the effect of making us aware of the expressive qualities of film and the actors' performances.

*Feltham Sings* features a handful of individuals who tell their stories in naturalistic close-ups in their cells. They are then seen performing musical numbers in which they voice their thoughts and feelings about their crimes and life inside. Stylistically, these 'numbers' range from rap to reggae to hip-hop, while shooting, lighting and camerawork pitch their performance between the naturalistic style of the interviews and the aesthetics of the pop video. During the numbers, the placement of the performer – literally behind bars as one sings of incarceration, through a cell peephole as another sings of constant eavesdropping – helps to shape what we see just as in a feature film or TV drama. The 'scratch video' look contributes to the 'authenticity' of underprivileged street life, according to a convention TV programmes, films and pop videos have made recognizable. The use of fisheye lenses exaggerates the cramped nature of prison life. Split screens show inmates in apparently adjacent 'cells' in one scene; two inmates seem to be walking together until we catch on to the split screen effect. In between songs, the camera prowls around the corridors and rooms of the prison, making us feel like inmates.

Deploying a range of filmic and performative conventions as it does, we have to ask to what extent this style of documentary departs from the nitty gritty of real experience. Displaying the performative documentary's apparent privileging of style over experience, *Feltham Sings* is, arguably, a pretty cool programme.

## Reality TV

For some, reality TV has come to embody the big nationwide audiences that tuned into BBC1 and ITV before satellite, cable TV, and domestic cinema options became available. Its minute-by-minute record of life in the *Big Brother* (Channel 4, 2000–) house may seem desperately uninteresting to some, but it is *Big Brother*'s very ordinariness that got people watching, then talking about it. As we follow the action from room to room, we see and hear things individual participants do not see or hear. Being one step ahead makes gossip even juicier. Unlike documentary, we know that *Big Brother* is thoroughly contrived. This is not real accommodation. These are not real friends. They are only here for the money. But its appeal depends on its similarity to everyday experience. Short-term projects, constant appraisal, ruthless management – this is what the British workplace has become for large numbers of *Big Brother* viewers. But where does the fun and games of *Big Brother* end and real work begin? Reality TV such as *The Salon* homes in on the public and private business of a real hair salon. Following it, you stand to learn as much about the work of a salon as you might about the life of mammals by watching David Attenborough. Interviewed in 2001, Christopher Hird, Managing Director of Fulcrum TV and chair of the Sheffield International Documentary Festival, realized that the line between reality TV and documentary is blurring all the time. 'As programme-makers, we want to make broadcasts that get watched, or make waves, or expand the range of what's possible – or all three, if we can manage it.'

## Crime drama

Crime dramas on British TV fall largely into three categories, although there is a degree of hybridization. The earliest to develop was the traditional genre, a format established in the 1950s with *Dixon of Dock Green* (BBC, 1950–75) and the US series *Dragnet* (1952–59). In this type a small group of detectives tackled and resolved a particular case each week. Each episode followed the actions of characters embodying an unblemished brand of heroism. Appearing to have no personal lives, these characters revolved around their work. Meanwhile, the criminals, remote from the audience and not developed beyond a few obvious traits, were always caught or killed. Camerawork tended to depict the world in the orderly

*'The shows I make tend to be real people in real situations, though constructed by us. A pure reality show is a planned fiction, a quasi-anthropological experiment. It's precinct TV with people on an island or in a Big Brother container.'* (Channel 4 Editorial Director Daisy Goodwin, 2001, The Guardian, 25 July 2001)

▶ Whose house is the *Big Brother* house? Why are we watching these people? Does having an audience change anything? ●

style of magazine photography: nicely framed, no odd angles, regular lighting. In this style individual shots establish clearly what is going on. Used sparingly, dramatic lighting and angles help to generate heightened involvement and tension. In the traditional crime drama, respectable professionals are portrayed as defending respectable society from crime against the backdrop of a recognizable everyday reality.

At the close of each episode of *Dixon of Dock Green*, PC Dixon would approach the camera in a dark street and tell us how that week's particular case was resolved. Airing in prime-time evening slots, the impression sought was of your local bobby standing on your street and reassuring you that the world was safe again. This form of direct address is not used now. But a contemporary series such as *A Touch of Frost* (ITV, 1992–2004) does feature an authoritative figure conversing with colleagues about motives and methods in such a way as to explain what is going on and to reassure the middle-class audience that the world is in safe hands. He may be unconventional or mysterious in his methods, but DI Frost, like the police in *Dixon of Dock Green*, represents a God-like moral order watching over us. If in recent years the crimes in *A Touch of Frost* have become increasingly violent and apparently senseless, this suggests the programme's attempt to come to terms with a society which seems to the average person to grow more violent and unpredictable with every passing day. It also signalled the inflection of this strand of crime drama by the psychodramas that emerged in the 1990s.

Psychodramas such as *Cracker* (ITV, 1993–96) and *Trial and Retribution* (ITV, 1997–2004) appeared partly in response to the shift towards the gruesome and the psychological in the big screen thriller typified by *The Silence of the Lambs* (Jonathan Demme, 1990) and *Seven* (David Fincher, 1995). One of the conventions of this strand is the troubled hero, a character with personal problems that make him difficult to work with. Fitz in *Cracker* is a forensic psychiatrist whose insights into the criminal mind seem inextricably linked to his own complex persona. The psychodrama uses low key light and split screens to generate an aura of the menacing nature of contemporary crime and its detection.

Produced by Tony Garnett, associated with Ken Loach's realist dramas of the 1960s, *Buried* (Channel 4, 2003) focuses on the psychological traumas of men in prison. Lacking the

The Bill: *a tangle of rotating narratives*

morally authoritative centre of the traditional crime drama, *Buried* is unafraid of the dark side of human nature. Shot in natural light made dull by concrete walls and bars, and employing a long-take camera style and extreme close-ups before often violent and painful mental disintegration, *Buried* is propelled by dialogue rich in character and vernacular and often obscene. With no music, and steeped in naturalistic sound even over the credits – clanging doors, screams in the night – the world depicted has no clear paths between right and wrong. Like the neo-noir films that influenced it, the emphasis in the psychodrama is on the inner lives of men, rather than women characters. Notice how public information messages for helplines follow the programme, suggesting its purchase on real experience.

The other strand of crime drama is the soap opera, a mode in which personal problems are examined in close detail. Indeed, the soap opera format exploring the work-life balance is common to much TV drama from *Casualty* (BBC1, 1986–) to *Attachments* (BBC2, new media, 2000–). In soap opera-style series such as *The Bill* (ITV, 1983–) and *Merseybeat* (BBC1, 2001–04), episodes revolve around the work and personal lives of busy police stations. In neither series do we witness the perpetration of crimes nor get to know the criminals in any depth. Like the police, we can be taken in by them, but invariably the criminals and witnesses the police come into contact with are one-dimensional, the actors often making the most of their tics. The effect finds us seeming to uncover the truth as the police do. Like soap opera, episodes feature a tangle of rotating narratives around the characters' work challenges, love lives, money worries etc. Characters discuss each other in the way viewers discuss soap opera characters, conferring real-life status on fictional characters. By asking his partner why a member of the public is behaving oddly, a detective involves us in the solution of the case.

This type of crime drama tends to feature a range of ethnic minorities. As in a soap opera such as *EastEnders*, the issues are often of a topical nature. In *The Bill* we hear that a child has been gunned down in a drug war, evoking contemporary British concerns over gun crime. A characteristic of the soap opera-style crime drama is anger and frustration as the police find themselves trying to protect the public against increasingly senseless violence in the wider world, but are constricted by regulations and cutbacks which seem equally senseless. Visually, the look is cramped, the focus on talking heads amid drab station interiors and unremarkable urban exteriors. *Merseybeat* is set somewhere on Merseyside. *The Bill* is set in a Metropolitan Police station in a fictional inner London borough. Occasionally, when the action demands it, the camera is hand-held. Otherwise, the filming style finds the camera at human's eye view while camera and cutting follow the action, conforming to what we describe as an everyday 'objective' view of the world.

## Soap opera

Of all the TV genres, the soap opera is regarded as a key realist enterprise. Julia Smith, the creator of *EastEnders* (1985–), has compared the programme with Charles Dickens's episodic realist novels of ninetheenth-century East End life. Describing *EastEnders* as 'documentary realism', Smith links this most popular British soap opera to the most hallowed tradition of British film-making. First airing in 1985, key *EastEnders* episodes have captured 60 per cent of the total British terrestrial and satellite TV audience. (*Coronation Street*'s (ITV, 1960–) share is around 56 per cent; *Emmerdale*'s (ITV, 1972–) is nearer 54 per cent.)

We may think that a drama depicting the everyday lives of everyday characters represents the height of realism; however, soap operas are as contrived and constructed as any other programme on television. Watch carefully and you will notice that you are constantly being cued to think and react to characters not only by their dialogue, but also by the camera and the cutting. On the one hand, a single line of dialogue and the shot/reverse-shot cutting can lead us to believe Little Mo has met another man behind the bar at the Queen Vic, triggering the perception that the script is deliberately manipulating us. On the other, as Alfie Moon scuppers Kat's hopes for their marriage – 'It's not meant to be' – the producers want us to think that characters are in thrall to life's ups and downs, as we all are.

You will have noticed how melodramatic and emotional soap opera episodes can get. Soap opera has descended from a long tradition of TV drama having its roots in nineteenth- and early twentieth-century stage melodrama. As lifelike as they may seem, adultery, divorce, shady pasts and fatal

▶ Compare the kind of story told in a 'realistic' soap opera with the kind of story told in *Rome, Open City* (1945) or *Kandahar* (2001). In what ways do these kinds of storytelling differ? ●

EastEnders: *what's meant to be . . .*

illnesses do not happen in real life with quite the frequency that they occur in Albert Square or Coronation Street!

Have you noticed how soap operas tend to be set in distinctive communities in which the characters all know each other? *EastEnders* is set in and around Albert Square in the fictitious east London borough of Walford. *Coronation Street* (ITV) is set in and around a fictitious street in Manchester. As the various plots rotate among the characters, there is always enough interaction with the world of the square or the street that we recognize this community as belonging to the same world as our community. As fictitious as Albert Square and Coronation Street are, we are able to suspend our disbelief in order to relate to it. *EastEnders* reinforces its realism by making the most of its exteriors. The public space of the market stalls and the Queen Vic pub, a typical London pub façade, act as places where these East End types would interact. Hence, we never question the verisimilitude of locations that, in fact, do not exist. This narrative space becomes unquestionably part of the drama as we see characters inhabiting it. A character whose story we followed a moment ago is seen over someone's shoulder, for example, each edition roving between narrative strands even on the same set. One conversation takes place down the bar from another involving characters we were with a moment ago. Notice how the editing seems to 'stitch' you into the space as well as the drama by positioning the viewer as a bystander in close proximity to the characters as they talk. It is as if you live in Albert Square and happen to be in the vicinity.

As in real experience, the soap opera plot is open-ended, occurring in the 'infinite middle' rather than having a beginning, middle and an end. Moving from one plot to another, the soap opera catches that real sense we have that our lives go on and on, one situation being resolved and setting up the conditions for the next. The only endings occur as characters either leave the community or die off. Cliffhangers are vital. Character emphases shift constantly. Following Tariq's donation of his kidney to Ronny, and Tariq's acceptance as part of the Ferreira family, emphasis shifted to his half-brother Adi's struggle to come to terms with their father's resentment towards him. In the soap opera, as in life, experience is a tapestry of events and outcomes. This experiential aspect also has the effect of dividing the audience. Much of the popular discussion of soap operas revolves around audience opinions about particular characters. In the 1980s the furore over Dirty Den was reported in the tabloids so assiduously that you could have been forgiven for thinking that he was a real person! By 2003, Janine Butcher had become Albert Square's villainess.

Notice, too, how plots seem to expand rather than unfold in a linear fashion. When Charlie Slater found out that his daughter Kat had betrayed him by paying off her sister Little Mo's rapist, he scorns and rejects Kat. Meanwhile, when Kat's husband, Alfie, asks if she would be happy for Alfie's Nana and her beau to live with them after their marriage, Kat agrees wholeheartedly, thereby signalling a shift in Kat's allegiances from her biological family to a 'family' of her own. Very little actually *happens* in this story strand. Our interest in it was sustained by revelations by one character about another. This device is used constantly to focus on character itself and move the narrative along. Soap operas provide a training ground for actors, and revelations bring other dimensions to their performances and offer them the opportunity to stretch themselves.

As in a million novels and films, irony is a constant in *EastEnders*. As Phil Mitchell throws young Jamie out of his house, we get a close-up of a holly wreath declaring 'Goodwill to All Men' on the wall. Ask yourself why the director chose to emphasize this feature of the *mise-en-scène*. Music is used for dramatic resonance. When Laura finds the paperwork relating to Ian's attempt to gain control of their fish and chip shop, we hear 'Don't Get Me Wrong' by the Pretenders on the soundtrack.

Aimed at a younger audience, *Hollyoaks* (Channel 4/E4, 1995–) and *Brookside* (Channel 4, 1982–2003) often use black-and-white footage for flashbacks, hand-held cameras and canted angles, devices familiar from pop videos and thrillers. By comparison, the camera style and cutting on *EastEnders* tends to be more conservative. But like the dramatic devices, the camerawork is no less designed to get a response or engender a specific interpretation. Most soap opera episodes end on a close-up of a character as a climax occurs. Ask yourself how often you get to see even people you know well in such an intimate way.

Aimed at young people, *Hollyoaks* tends to focus on moral issues relating to sex, relationships, drugs and delinquency.

▶ Compare the style of *Hollyoaks* with that of *Dangerous Minds*. ●

Aimed at working people, *EastEnders* focuses on issues relating to money and work, marriage and relationships. Trading in these everyday dramas, soap operas offer viewers the opportunity to sort out right from wrong in their own minds. You are constantly being invited to side with or against a particular character in some moral dispute. Adhering to screenwriting conventions perhaps, characters seem to come ready-made with flaws built in. Yet how many of us, if we are honest, tend to react to situations in habitual ways and without thinking? Soap operas give friends, neighbours and workmates talking points.

Not just a form of emotional pornography, as some commentators have described them, they bring in topical issues. Notice how public information messages advertising AIDS or homelessness helplines relevant to the plots often follow soap opera episodes, reinforcing the programme's purchase upon a real Britain. However, if the topicality becomes too controversial, viewers may become alienated. The firemen's strike was used as background in *EastEnders*, for example, although it was not overtly discussed. The Iraq War was not even mentioned.

In an era when communities and families have apparently become less important or prominent in our lives, the artificial communities of Albert Square and Brookside offer focus for a Britain which seems to have degenerated into a mass of competing individuals. Soap operas in turn generate artificial communities among viewers, united only by following soap operas. There is constant negotiation between regarding characters as real and realizing that they and the programme are contrived. The *EastEnders* website solicits fans with gimmicks that assume a real community history and those that inform about the production of *EastEnders*. On the one hand, you can vote for your 'neighbour from hell'. On the other, you can read interviews with Jessie Wallace (Kat) and Shane Richie (Alfie). Click a button and you can 'Take a Sneaky Look around Walford', or 'Win a Tour of Albert Square'. *Hollyoaks*'s less sophisticated site contains all the newsy and chatty content-based prompts, but does not invite the fan to reflect upon the characters as *characters*, the soap opera as *programme*. This may be because, unlike *EastEnders*, *Hollyoaks* has yet to become an institution, a piece of TV history. The *EastEnders* site, by comparison, acknowledges that soap opera fans are now increasingly sophisticated.

Traditionally, all characters in soap operas tend to conform to stock models designed to elicit stock audience responses. But the very typicality of the communities depicted in soap operas can also be an index of their artificiality. Trading in lovable rogues (Alfie Moon), pushy street vendors (Mo Slater) and jolly Jamaicans (Patrick), does *EastEnders* present us with real people or Cockney archetypes? Once upon a time there were no characters from racial minorities in soap operas. Now some of the most interesting characters in *EastEnders* and *Coronation Street* are of Afro-Caribbean or Asian descent. While it is true that many soap opera characters are more complex, for many Nana Moon is still Hilda Braid, the veteran of countless British comedy films and TV series since the 1960s, a reminder of British realism's heritage.

▶ Compare Lindsay Anderson's *Every Day Except Christmas* with an episode of *EastEnders*. ●

## Comedy

*The Office* (BBC, 2001–2003) was an attempt to catch the dynamics of life in a typical British office. Featuring the 'types' that all office workers have at one time or another met – self-important manager, overeducated underling, sexy receptionist – the programme has tapped into the reality of working life for millions of people. Employing an unobtrusive shooting style, naturalistic acting, and catching even dead time, *The Office* invites us to witness funny, cringe-making, sometimes even poignant moments as the personnel expose their weaknesses. Much comedy revolves around the discrepancy between self-image and the perceptions of others. Because *The Office* steeped this perennial human comedy in the manners and mores of contemporary British society, the minutiae of a rolling camera, the programme makes its characters all the more poignant. Manager David Brent sees himself as a renaissance man, adept at all the civilized arts and best friend to the workforce. But he comes across as egotistical and tactless, and he continually insults the female staff. Gareth sees himself as intelligent and efficient, and great with women. As we watch his exchanges with Tim and others, he comes across as petty and stupid. Receptionist Dawn fancies Tim, and their own 'Will they? Won't they?' rapport, surreptitiously played out against the backdrop of other dynamics, was itself complex and ambiguous. Among the most telling, and funny, moments in *The Office* was the episode in which David launches into a dance routine for Red Nose Day. When a new girl starts, Gareth takes her under his wing. Commandeering David's office as if it were his own, Gareth gives her a health and safety tour, teaching her, among other things, how to sit down and stand up safely! The episode in which David delays the revelation of redundancies is excruciating, exploring as it does contemporary anxieties around job security and social credibility.

*Jam* (Channel 4, 2003) is a sketch-format comedy in which familiar situations such as undergoing an interview or visiting the doctor are subverted by the introduction of warped, surreal moments. While the use of conventions such as a straight man, a funny man and punchlines suggests contrivance, surveillance footage, hand-held DV and voice-overs confer a realist patina. The unethical doctor and the documentary of the recluse who makes friends by causing mishaps to passers-by are typical of *Jam*'s project of playing on everyday British social embarrassment. It is symptomatic of their relevance to the contemporary status quo that *Jam* and *Brass Eye* ran for one season, then disappeared.

▶ Why is so much British comedy – from Mike Leigh to *Jam* – based around embarrassment? ●

# 7. And Finally ... Digital Reality

*An overview of the impact that new media are having on our perceptions of the image, narrative and the world around us, Chapter 7 looks briefly at the practical and theoretical implications of interactivity. In perhaps the ultimate acknowledgment that moving images offer a world mediated by their makers, Internet-based conspiracy games spill over into the player's own life. The Web is a treasure trove of facts and images. But who controls the Web?*

The vast majority of films and television programmes that we have looked at so far have been produced involving the photographic recording of real experience. As we have already seen, however, digital imaging is becoming increasingly prevalent in the cinema and on television. In the closing years of the twentieth century, the Web, computer games and multimedia came to dominate leisure time, shaping our perceptions of the moving image and its relationship with reality. But how are the Web and image-capture techniques altering these perceptions?

The key difference between these new media and traditional moving-image media is that we interact with new media much more obviously than we do with old media. Traditionally, when we went to the cinema we went to watch a preformed narrative that does not change and which unfolds before a passive audience. By contrast, when we sit before a computer monitor surfing the Net or playing a computer game, we can control what we see and how and

'Moving between two and three dimensions, between fiction and fact, between imagination and observation, between memory and desire, between illusion and reality, cinema flickers on the interface of the real and the simulated: in this, it may not only be a prototype of the moving image, but also of the strangeness of digital culture itself.' (Nicolas Tredell in Cinemas of the Mind, p. 235)

where the session will end. If the audience in the cinema has a collective experience because each person saw the same film, the solitary surfer or game-player has a unique and distinctive experience each time he or she sits down.

If you think about it, the photochemical technology that brought us photography, then motion photography in the nineteenth century, resulted in as much technological manipulation of experience as does digital imaging. Since the Lumières the cinema has seen an assortment of techniques of image manipulation from models and mattes to optical effects and rear projection. Should new media, therefore, prompt us to ask new questions about how we make sense of imaged experience?

Well, no and yes! At the institutional and aesthetic levels, films and video games share a lot in common. As we have seen, for some time computer-generated imagery has been turning up in Hollywood blockbusters, while video games rely upon the generic and visual conventions of Hollywood sci-fi movies and thrillers, as well as Japanese manga movies. The instances of games being made into movies finds the traffic going both ways. If one-dimensional characterizations have tended to betray the relative immaturity of the computer game, games are becoming increasingly sophisticated. Around the turn of the century, second-generation PlayStation machines began to incorporate real-time representations and surround sound that mimics multiplex auditorium sound. Game designers constantly seek to combine a cinematic feel in the graphics with the illusion of freedom that interactivity brings between player and game. Aside from concerns about violent content that characterized the evolution of the video game just as they did film and then video, a regular criticism of computer games has been their depiction of gender. The prevalence of male programmers and game developers resulted in fewer games aimed at women; however, this is changing. While Lara Croft made an appeal to the girl game-player on the basis of physical empowerment and ability to compete in a male world, games promoting mental agility, wit and interpersonal skills are emerging to appeal to the female game-player. The world of the traditional video game may share a male bias in common with the Hollywood boardroom and multiplex line-up, but games are gradually growing up.

If the real-world experience that has moulded our experience of the movies remains relevant to the experience of playing a computer game, interactivity brings fresh poignancy to the game developers' attempt to make the game world more real. A number of theorists have discussed the issues raised by interactivity. The immediacy, or 'presence', of the game world, as opposed to the mediated reality of traditional image media, has been hotly discussed. Another aspect of the gaming experience is that of participation in the game, as opposed to our passive manipulation before the cinema screen. Virtual realities are ongoing, incomplete, as opposed to the finished narrative of a film. That the player is always already involved in shaping the course and outcome of the game is caught in what has been termed the 'subjunctive state', a state of what could have been rather than what was or will be, as in the finished narrative of a film.

As we have seen, the virtual reality (VR) headset immerses the wearer in the dimensions of a virtual world. VR moves beyond the 'window on the world' traditionally promised by films and TV programmes, promising a 'door into the world', as it were. Moving a step further, the world of the Internet-based interactive conspiracy game *Majestic* actually invades the real world of the player. Dependent not upon the representations of virtual world characters and events as is the average computer game, *Majestic* requires that the player register and become enlisted in the search for fugitives missing since a game company was infiltrated. Like the protagonist in the feature film *The Game* (David Fincher, 1997), the player is surprised by e-mails and strange events. Parallel worlds, in the shape of 'Web universes' designed to accompany films and TV series, have begun to appear that contain intricate, apparently true, data to back up the claims made by the programme. In the conspiracy mockumentary *Nothing So Strange* (Brian Flemming, 2002), we are taken into a fictional 1999 in which Microsoft's Bill Gates is gunned down before our eyes. You can then investigate a complex Web ring of sites relating to the investigation, and even contribute to the growing conspiracy around Gates's 'death'.

Whether seen as a cornucopia of information, opinion and opportunity, or as a frivolous and dangerous distraction, the Web is a window on the world in living rooms and bedrooms all over the world. Consisting of countless websites dedicated

The sci-fi movie *Strange Days* (Kathryn Bigelow, 1995) brings a controversial dimension to the possibilities of headset immersion through the hypothetical SQUID (Superconducting Quantum Interference Device) through which the wearer can 'lock into' the multi-sensory consequences of another person's experience. At one point the hero, Lenny Nero, witnesses a woman's rape from the rapist's and the victim's perspective.

▶ *The Game* is a good example of a film becoming a metaphor for the film itself. While the constructedness of the film can be felt in the twists and turns of the game, you are put in the position of the unwitting player witnessing those twists and turns. Can you think of another film that pulls off this metaphorical assignment? What are the implications of this for the film's representation of experience? ●

to a daily increasing deluge of activities and endeavour, the Web enables us to learn an enormous amount about human experience. While it may seem to be dominated by major interests such as AOL, Yahoo and Lycos, the Web also contains a massive range of sites representing the lives and interests of factions, lobby groups and individuals with something to say about human experience. Although we must certainly be a little circumspect about some of the claims that we find there, nevertheless, driven by links from one site to the next, the 'narrative' we generate as we surf modifies our outlooks with each passing day.

## Summary

Issues around realism go to the very nature of the moving image because what we see on screen is both real, as it was once in front of the camera, and fake, as the process of filming changes what it was. All realisms, from the narrative realism of Hollywood to the naturalism of Iranian films, from the quirky record of the US indie to the 'documentary realism' of *EastEnders*, are both intimately involved in real experience *and* irrevocably removed from everyday life. Never has realism been so vital to a consideration of aesthetics as it has been since the development of film and television. The advent of new media, with its attendant interactivity, has only enhanced the role of realist aesthetics in moving-picture texts.

Yet because the interaction between record and rendition, between the documentary pole of the Lumières and the fantasy pole of Méliès, is so complex, we must paradoxically talk about *effects* of truth and reality when we discuss realist texts. A key part of the discussion we have about an individual film or television programme revolves around the genre, tradition or movement to which it belongs. By discussing these, we are ostensibly making a statement about the style of the film or television programme. But we are also talking about the degree to which effects contribute to the representation of real experience. Truth and reality effects are intricately related to and involved with aspects of a text's artifice such that to discuss its realism is simultaneously to discuss its aesthetics. Realism is an 'ism', just as surrealism and modernism are. As we have seen, while the mainstream romantic comedy looks like everyday life, its timelessness and its romantic conceit seem to remove the action and take it to a parallel universe. This is why a film's realism draws us in when we watch it, yet in hindsight the film seems self-contained, an interlude in the flow of experience not unlike a dream. (Indeed, some writers have treated watching films as akin to the experience of dreaming.)

Seeming to mimic real life more honestly, the US indie film is just as involved in parodying Hollywood, as well as elaborating on its own aesthetics. Counter cinemas such as those emerging during the 1960s have also employed a range of devices to interrogate mainstream film-making and to reveal its ideological assumptions. While genre provides a prism through which we see how individual Hollywood films work through issues of representation, independent and experimental work reflects upon how genres themselves operate to represent experience.

Behind any text's representations are its ideological assumptions, and behind these lie the play of economic, political and social pressures that shape all cultural production, but most emphatically the moving-image media. Examine any text on the level of its marketing and exhibition, and on the level of its textual operations, and ideological assumptions become increasingly obvious. Censorship has played a key role in film history, not only restricting and shaping what can be seen, but actively promoting certain messages and particular kinds of films as well.

Historically, the emergence of realisms around the world has tended to coincide with changes in a country's political climate involving a shift towards liberal regimes. This happened in Italy at the end of World War II, in Britain in the 1960s, in Iran in the 1990s. Invariably, realist aesthetics pushed out the boundaries of what can be shown and discussed in films and television programmes, these movements characterized by their revelation of hidden histories. Yet realist new waves have also tended towards a male bias, leading to a bias in their revelatory project, and revealing their loaded outlook.

Realism has been particularly relevant to the long-running debate around whether British cinema should emulate Hollywood imports or try for a homegrown alternative arising out of the facts and conditions of British life. One notion of British cinema has been institutionally and aesthetically related to British television. Realism has

▶ A number of important developments in film history have occurred in particular countries during tumultuous moments in their history – Germany following World War I and the United States in the 1970s, for example. Can you think of any reason why a cinematic renaissance might be related to historical upheaval? ●

▶ How has studying realism made you more aware of your own role in making meaning? In what ways? ●

traditionally been key to British television, in particular its documentaries, soap operas and current affairs coverage. But however much television draws upon British society for its content, its aesthetics still shape how we see what we watch. Perhaps the television news is the most immediate window on the world. Nevertheless, to watch the news closely is to witness the extent to which the moving-image media conceal, as well as reveal, the world around us. As audiences become increasingly aware of their manipulation, programme makers, film-makers and game designers become shrewder in their attempts to keep the boundary between experience and artifice fluid and interesting. Meanwhile, does our thirst for realistic moving images say more about real experience or more about us?

# Glossary

**actualités** A French term originally used to describe the short documentary records filmed by the Lumière brothers in the 1890s. Literally translated as 'current events', nowadays *les actualités* is used in France to refer to the news, or to cinema and television generally.

**aesthetics** A set of principles of taste and the appreciation of beauty. In film, aesthetics refers to all those methodologies and techniques that transform real experience into a film's representation of that experience. Everything that conditions the way we see what we see, from the director directing the actor to the tweaking of the image during laboratory development, comes under aesthetics. Collectively, a film's aesthetics describe the manner and extent of its representation of experience.

**alienation** When a film becomes difficult to follow, it can be because it employs devices that deliberately distance you from the identification and immersion that you expect from a film. This distancing alienates you, but enables you to examine the film's ideological assumptions more easily.

**auteurism** A method of film analysis based on the assumption that a single individual, usually the director, is responsible for the aesthetic character of a film. Auteurism's implications for realist film-making consist in the singularity of the director's version of experience and the degree to which it involves the aesthetic transformation of reality.

**censorship** Any attempt to alter or suppress a film by governments or other agencies using an appeal to notions of the public good. Censorship impinges upon realism in cases in which films depicting aspects of experience deemed subversive are affected. For example, during the 'video nasty' debate in Britain in the mid 1990s, films were targeted that were supposedly behind 'copycat' crimes. Dominant groups use censorship to promote particular aesthetics and content.

**cinéma-vérité** A French documentary movement of the early 1960s, the term is now used more loosely to describe films or movements which attempt to capture raw experience in an unmediated way. Films as disparate as the Free Cinema shorts, the Danish Dogme films, and *The Blair Witch Project* (1999) have been termed *cinéma-vérité*.

**distanciation** The process by which the spectator is alienated from a film in order to facilitate questioning of its ideological and aesthetic assumptions.

**docudrama** A film or TV programme in which a record of real-world events and characters is depicted as drama, using actors and a script. Such films seek to entertain while achieving historical accuracy and authenticity. *Schindler's List* (Steven Spielberg, 1993) and *Ali* (Michael Mann, 2001) are examples of docudrama.

**documentary** A film or TV record of real world events and characters the realist implications of which are called into question by the degree of intervention between the camera and the event. Arguably, the purest record of experience is found in observational documentaries. The most self-conscious record is found in the performative type. Other types of documentary – expository, interactive, poetic, reflexive – represent degrees of intervention that draw attention to the impossibility of an unmediated record of reality.

**docu-soap** A TV programme that revolves around a group of characters brought together by a shared endeavour such as working together in a hair salon, crossing the Kalahari Desert, or taking driving lessons.

**facticity** The condition of being in the world. A thing's facticity is its irreducible 'is-ness'. The realism of a realist text depends upon its ability to engender a sense of real existence.

**genre** A type or category of moving image text (e.g. thriller, Western, crime drama, soap opera). Consisting of distinctive conventions of representation, genres play a key role in shaping the portrayal of experience in a film or TV programme.

**ideology** The system of ideas and beliefs that underlies a society and the cultural texts that it produces. Moving-image texts are suffused with ideology on an explicit and an implicit level. The prevalence of romantic scenarios in Hollywood films, for example, implies a society which values individual fulfilment and 'family values', itself a loaded term carrying ideological assumptions. Clues as to a film's explicit ideological character can be found in its trailer or on its poster. Clues as to its implicit ideological character can be found by examining the film as a film.

**interactivity** The mode of engagement between a computer game player and the game, and the Web surfer and the Internet. This mode has a number of implications for the way in which computer games and Internet sites represent experience, as well as for the way we experience interactivity.

**naturalism** Originally a literary aesthetic that represents experience as natural process, employing detailed reportage and 'scientific' documentation to generate the impression of objectivity. In film-making, natural light, location shooting and long takes typify this style. Examples of naturalism include Mike Leigh's portraits of English life or *EastEnders*; however, to the extent that they fail to tackle the contradictions that lie beneath social and political processes, naturalist films and television can be as contrived as any other text.

**new media** A term covering computer games, the Internet, DVD and digital television and video.

**New Wave** A term used to characterize emergent generations of film-making. While New Waves have increased the cinema's ability to represent experience, these realisms have tended to privilege the experiences and attitudes of men.

**overloading** When a film deliberately generates the impression that it contains significance, then undermines this impression. Relevant to experimental and arthouse traditions already loaded with critical and audience expectations, overloading tends to distance the spectator.

**patriarchy** A status quo that privileges men and masculine attitudes. Traditionally, most societies have been patriarchal, and their cinemas have reflected this. In recent decades, career girl and action heroine archetypes in Hollywood films, and independent women in arthouse cinema, have increasingly challenged patriarchal assumptions.

**political correctness** An ideology that became fashionable in the United States and Britain in the 1990s which represented the attempt to combat negative racial and cultural stereotyping. Politically correct representations of racial and cultural minorities now find their way into Hollywood films and US network TV shows on a regular basis.

**propaganda** A programme of publicity or selection of information designed to propagate a particular doctrine or practice. Film has been a powerful tool of propaganda, and has been used by governments to promote particular ideologies and policies. But, arguably, the most subtle and successful form of propaganda in the history of the world has been Hollywood cinema.

**reality effect** When a moving-image text generates an effect that is consistent with reality. For example, when a scene set in a recognizable London location contains a number of black cabs. Conversely, if a scene set in a recognizable London location featured yellow New York cabs this would not be consistent with reality.

**reality TV** A genre of actuality TV in which real-time activities are monitored by surveillance cameras, hidden microphones and broadcast with minimum editing. *Big Brother* (2000 et al.) remains perhaps the most popular British example.

**representation** Broken down, the term 're-presentation' refers to the way in which moving-image texts *re*-present experience. As indicated by its constituent parts, representation refers to both the method of representation and what is represented. The act of representing experience in a moving-image text implies the use of codes and conventions that are never completely free of ideological associations.

**truth effect** When a moving-image text generates an effect that is consistent with what we believe about reality. For example, when we see a tearful woman in a film pushing her way through a crowd at an accident we may assume that it is someone's mother because she is acting in a way that is consistent with how mothers behave when their children are harmed.

**underfilling** When a film generates impressions that give the spectator few clues about what is going on or how they are meant to interpret events. Usually relevant to the experimental or arthouse traditions in which this strategy is used to distance the spectator.

**verisimilitude** The appearance of being true. Embodying reality and truth effects, the verisimilitude of a film or TV programme refers to its ability to make the spectator believe that what they are watching has some purchase upon real experience.

# Further reading

## Chapter 1

Bazin, André, *What Is Cinema?*, vol. 1, edited by Hugh Gray (Berkeley: University of California Press, 1992).

Ellis, John, *Visible Fictions: Cinema, Television, Video* (London & New York: Routledge, 1992).

Nichols, Bill, *Representing Reality* (Bloomington: Indiana University Press, 1991).

Nochlin, Linda, *Realism* (Harmondsworth: Penguin, 1991).

## Chapter 2

Allen, Michael, *Contemporary US Cinema* (Harlow: Longman, 2003).

Biskind, Peter, *Down and Dirty Pictures: Miramax, Sundance and the Rise of Independent Film,* (London: Bloomsbury, 2004).

Bordwell, David, Janet Staiger & Kristin Thompson, *The Classical Hollywood Cinema: Film Style and Mode of Production to 1960* (London: Routledge, 1985).

Hillier, Jim (ed.), *American Independent Cinema: A Sight and Sound Reader* (London: British Film Institute, 2001).

King, Geoff, *New Hollywood Cinema: An Introduction* (New York: Columbia University Press, 2002).

Pierson, John, *Spike, Mike, Slackers and Dykes* (London: Faber, 1995).

## Chapter 3

Dick, Bernard F., *Anatomy of Film* (Basingstoke: Macmillan, 1998).

Evans, Peter William, & Celestino Deleyto (eds), *Terms of Endearment: Hollywood Romantic Comedy of the 1980s and 1990s* (Edinburgh: Edinburgh University Press, 1998).

King, Geoff, *Film Comedy* (London: Wallflower Press, 2002).

Saunders, John, *The Western Genre: From Lordsburg to Big Whiskey* (London: Wallflower Press, 2001).

## Chapter 4

Cook, Pam, & Mieke Bernink (eds), *The Cinema Book* (London: British Film Institute, 1999).

Light, Andrew, *Reel Arguments: Film, Philosophy and Social Criticism* (Boulder, Co, & Oxford: Westview, 2003).

Medved, Michael, *Hollywood vs America: Popular*

*Culture and the War against Traditional Values* (London: HarperCollins, 1992).

Turner, Graeme, *Film as Social Practice* (London & New York: Routledge, 1993).

## Chapter 6

Carney, Ray, & Leonard Quart, *The Films of Mike Leigh* (Cambridge: Cambridge University Press, 2000).

Cooke, Lez, *British Television Drama: A History* (London: British Film Institute, 2003.)

Higson, Andrew (ed.), *Dissolving Views: Key Writings on British Cinema* (London: Cassell, 1996).

Hill, John, *Sex, Class and Realism: British Cinema 1956–63* (London: British Film Institute, 1986).

Lay, Samantha, *British Social Realism: From Documentary to Brit Grit* (London: Wallflower Press, 2002).

Leigh, Jacob, *The Cinema of Ken Loach: Art in the Service of the People* (London: Wallflower Press, 2002).

Murphy, Robert (ed.), *British Cinema of the 90s* (London: BFI Publishing, 2000).

Robinson, Piers, *The CNN Effect: The Myth of News, Foreign Policy and Intervention* (London: Routledge, 2002).

Thussu, Daya Kishan, & Des Freedman (eds), *War and the Media: Reporting Conflict 24/7* (London: Sage, 2003).

Watson, Garry, *The Cinema of Mike Leigh: A Sense of the Real* (London: Wallflower Press, 2004).

Williamson, Judith, *Deadline at Dawn: Film Criticism 1980–1990* (London: Marion Boyars Publishers, 1993).

## Selected further reading

Black, Joel, *The Reality Effect: Film Culture and the Graphic Imperative* (London: Routledge, 2001).

Buckland, Warren, *Teach Yourself Film Studies* (London: Hodder & Stoughton, 1998).

Kochberg, Searle (ed.), *Introduction to Documentary Production: A Guide for Media Students* (London: Wallflower Press, 2002).

Tredell, Nicolas, *Cinemas of the Mind: A Critical History of Film Theory* (Cambridge: Icon, 2002).

# Index